The Lost Kingdom of PITTSBURGH

The Lost Kingdom of PITTSBURGH

A True Story of Art and Exile in the Steel City

by

KENNETH J. WEISS

AMERICA
THROUGH
TIME

America Through Time®
An imprint of Sutton Publishing Inc.
www.through-time.com

First published 2025

ISBN 978-1-63499-550-4

Typeset in 10pt on13pt Sabon
Printed and bound in England

Contents

Introduction

A Midrust Mystery

Tumbled within the Midwest and the Rust Belt, you will find places that are a little bit of both. Places where a short drive will take you from ubiquitous, withering towns to the homes of lost families and forgotten lands. You may think you know these places, but you don't. This is the Midrust.

The stories here are not just of fields and factories. The stories here are unexpected. Odd. Imaginative. Engaging.

The Midrust holds secrets—and this book is one of them

I have spent the last fifty years working, living, and writing in the Midrust. My day job has been helping brands tell stories through television, radio, video, print, and the endless facets of the digital realm. My spare time has been spent exploring the Midrust. I have chronicled over 1,000 stories for The Midrust Postcard Project (you can see the project on Instagram: @kennethjweiss).

The Midrust is the motivation and context for my novels, short stories, and now works of nonfiction. This area has such a story to tell. So much has never been said, and the stories continue to take shape.

Gibsonia, Pennsylvania

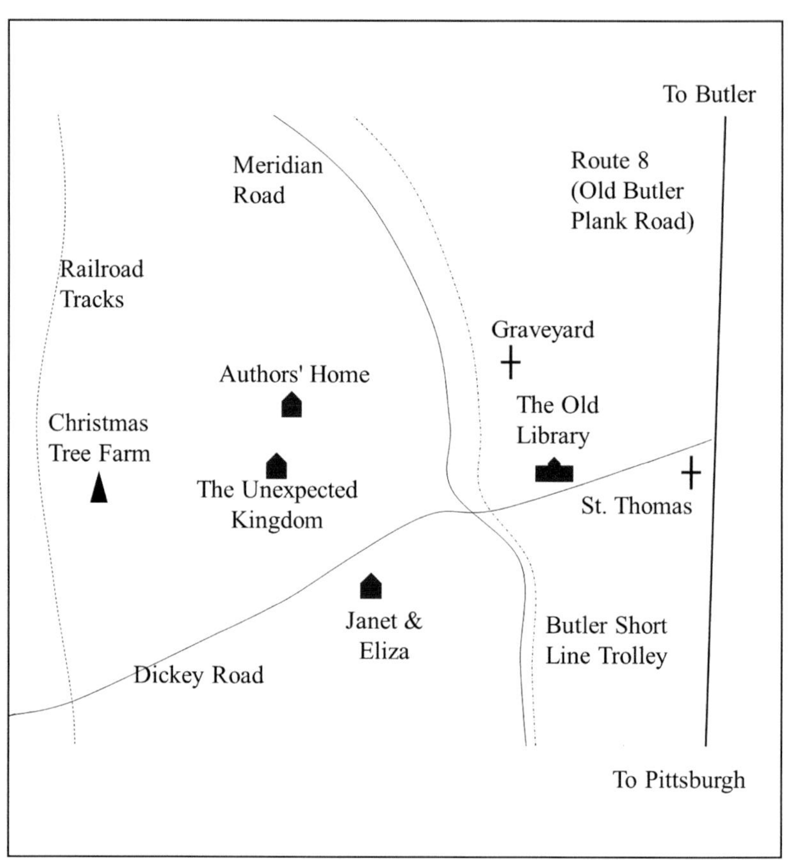

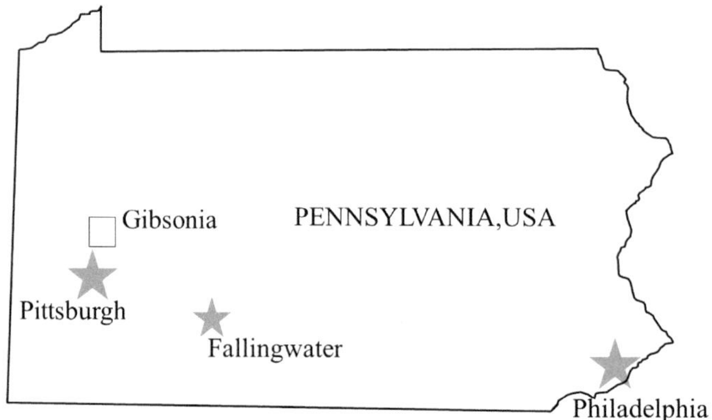

Note: Not all roads shown on map.

China During WWII

The Burma Road as it existed during the majority of World War II.

1974, A Small Community Outside of Pittsburgh

The place that shaped my childhood has always been remarkably unremarkable. Gibsonia, Pennsylvania, was the perfect example of a Midrust town: part Midwest, part Rust Belt. Our community was dotted with barns and farms, and many of the neighborhood dads commuted into Pittsburgh each morning for work. They returned at night with stories of struggling steel mills, rising inflation, gas shortages, and labor unrest.

Our particular neighborhood was carved from land that once made up the McKelvy farm. The lots were generous, and many were still empty when I was a kid. The houses that stood were built in the 1950s and '60s and were mostly ranch homes and split levels. One or two could be described as mid-century modern, and colonials were rare (only one or two). The whole thing was ordinary.

The fringes of our neighborhood, however, were where the adventures began. We had a cemetery which took the children's game of "Ghosts in the Graveyard" to another level. A sheep farm marked the end of a long trail that ran through the woods. The path that cut to the town library was anchored by a house which still had chicken coops and, most notably, a chopping block often covered with feathers and blood. Not too far to the west, a Christmas tree farm could be found with a seemingly endless warren of trees. Beyond that was a set of railroad tracks where we would often line the rails with rows of pennies and wait for the train. Each penny, if you could find it after the train passed, would be flattened into a thin, oblong wafer of copper with old Abe stretched and distorted, barely recognizable. We had plenty of patches of woods to build treehouses and more than enough ponds for fishing.

Our world was beautiful and simple, but the Midrust had surprises: the neighborhood held a mystery. We found it one day when we ventured to the edge of our usual travels to follow a dead-end road to see where it would go. This is funny, of course, because a dead-end road by definition goes nowhere. I was the youngest in our group of neighborhood kids, and having no real vote in the matter, just went along.

We followed the road down a long hill and across a narrow bridge made of a small culvert carrying a crick under the road. (We called them cricks rather than creeks.) The road became narrower with each step, and the trees tightly hemmed the edges. The asphalt stopped, turned to gravel, and ended in a thick stand of trees. Not much to see. Until you turned to the right.

Tucked in the woods, out of sight from the rest of the world, was a driveway, and towering over the driveway was a massive arch. The sides were made of columns more than 3 feet thick, and they supported a roof of timbers and cylindrical tiles that stretched over the width of the driveway. The roof was flared with the corners tilting to the sky. Each column was painted in a brilliant red and adorned with a vertical row of characters. Chinese characters! It was a gateway to another time and place. Amazed, scared, intrigued? Yes, we were all of those things. So we did the only logical thing: we followed the driveway.

Stately evergreens about 12 feet high, precisely spaced and impeccably trimmed, lined the drive leading up a long, gentle slope. At the top of the rise, the scenery became even more spectacular. A brilliantly painted pagoda three levels tall reached into the sky. A house built of brick and stone featuring the same amazing roof style as the arch anchored the top of the hill. Had a dragon walked out of the woods, I would not have been more surprised.

A young woman appeared and asked us if we would like to see the property. She showed us a gate that was a perfect circle almost 7 feet tall—a moon gate. It stood between the house and a garage and revealed beautiful gardens. We saw a pond with fish and floating lilies. We walked through meticulous patches of lawn rimmed with bushes and flowers that were unlike anything we had ever seen.

The place and the day were truly magical.

Over the years and decades that followed, a series of owners came and went from the property. Each was increasingly unfriendly. Some were openly hostile. The woods surrounding the property became thicker, and the trees were tagged with a series of signs: "Posted," "Private Property," "No Trespassing," and "Beware of Dog." Stories even spread of a curious visitor being met with the barrel of a shotgun.

I tucked away my memories of this place for almost fifty years.

The McKelvy Farm in Gibsonia, Pennsylvania, 17 miles north of Pittsburgh as it appeared in the early 1900s. The farm's acreage stretched far to the left of this picture. (*Photo courtesy of the Richland Township Historical Society*)

Robert Milton McKelvy and wife, Weslyann, around 1907. Two of the streets in the neighborhood, Milton Drive and Weslyann Drive, are named for them. (*Photo courtesy of the Richland Township Historical Society*)

A well being drilled on the McKelvy farm. The author's childhood home would be built on the hill behind the well decades later. (*Photo courtesy of the Richland Township Historical Society*)

Two Years Ago, Gibsonia, Pennsylvania

A business trip gave me the opportunity to return to my childhood. The schedule allowed me to separate my Monday and Tuesday meetings with dinner at my old home with my father. He remains sharp and active and has kept himself busy and purposeful in his later years.

After dinner, I decided to go for a walk around the neighborhood. A few new houses had been built, but the place remains virtually unchanged. On a whim, I decided to follow the road to the dead-end street, and then to the end. As I approached the spot where the asphalt gave way to gravel, it was impossible not to notice the assortment of warning signs, some old, some new, but even more than had been there in the past.

At the end, I turned and looked for the arch. It was still there, but covered in a layer of vines. The characters had been scraped from the columns leaving only faded outlines. Some of the roof tiles were missing. The paint on the columns had faded to a chalky brick color. I looked up the driveway. Tree branches and leaves were strewn everywhere. The tidy evergreens that once lined the drive had grown to more than 30 feet tall. The branches were tangled and scraggly.

If I was amazed as a child, I was saddened as an adult.

At that moment, God put a message in my thoughts, so clear and consuming that no room for misunderstanding could fit: "Time is running out on this place. It has a wonderful story. Find it. Tell it."

I never could have imagined that the journey of this story would cover more than 8,000 miles and more than 125 years. It led me to some of the most amazing coincidences and to the most interesting events. The tapestry of people, both famous and unknown, who touch this story is remarkable. They demonstrate innumerable lessons of love, faith, creativity, and sacrifice.

The story of this place and the three remarkable people that created it is in the pages that follow.

Remarkably, all of it is true.

Kenneth J. Weiss
www.kennethjweiss.com

The arch as it appeared when I rediscovered it a few years ago.

1
The Lost Kingdom of Pittsburgh

1902, Anhui, China: Quentin

Nestled in southeast China, the Anhui province appears as if the pages of a cosmic storybook were ripped free and pasted onto Earth by a divine force. The Yellow Mountains offer oddly sculpted pine trees, cathedral-like rock structures, ethereal seas of mist, and thermal springs forced to the surface by incalculable pressures. Both the Yangtze and Huaihe rivers run east through the province giving life to agriculture, transportation, and commerce.

While the land is eternal, the province itself dates only to the seventeenth century. In the mid-1600s, the Qing Dynasty conquered China, and in 1666, Jiangsu and Anhui were split into separate provinces. The borders established then remain today.

The beauty of Anhui, however, was constantly tainted by political instability across the entire region.

In 1894, bitterness between China and Japan over control over Korea erupted, and the Qing Dynasty went to war with the Empire of Japan in what is now known as the First Sino-Japanese War. The war was a tragedy for China. In less than a year, 35,000 Chinese soldiers were killed or wounded. Japan's toll was fewer than 5,000. The conflict ended with the Treaty of Shimonoseki, in which China recognized the independence of Korea and ceded Taiwan, the adjoining Pescadores, and the Liaodong Peninsula in Manchuria to Japan.

In addition to the territorial gains, Japan received war reparations of 200 million taels of silver from China—about 260 million ounces, which is $5 billion in today's money. The Qing government also had to grant permission for Japanese ships to sail up the Yangtze River, manufacturing grants for Japanese companies to operate in Chinese ports, and the opening of four additional ports to Japanese trading vessels.

The world took notice, and Russia, France, and Germany intervened. All three, especially Russia, objected to Japan's seizure of the Liaodong Peninsula. They pressured Japan into relinquishing the peninsula to Russia, in exchange for 30 million taels of silver.

Just a few years later, resentment to foreign intervention in China escalated into an anti-foreign, anti-colonial, and anti-Christian uprising across northern China called the Yihetuan Movement, or the Boxer Rebellion.

The consequences within the country's own borders were brutal. Over 100,000 people died in the conflict, including thousands of Chinese Christians. Foreign Christians and missionaries were particularly targeted. In 1899, two priests were killed in a German mission by Boxers. In response, Kaiser Wilhelm II, the German leader at the time, dispatched German troops to the scene of the crime, which further angered the rebels. Missionaries were seen by Boxers as agents of the foreign powers and were blamed for flood, drought, and unexplained deaths. Sarah Alice Young, an American missionary, was killed in the Shanxi province northwest of Anhui. She was stabbed on the banks of the Yellow River and died in the arms of her husband, John Young, a fellow American. They had been married just over a year. Sarah and John were among 180 missionaries and their families slaughtered in the summer of 1900.

Contrary to the intent of the Boxers, foreign intervention increased, culminating in August 1900 with the capture of Beijing by foreign troops. In 1901, the conflict ended with the signing of the Boxer Protocol. Signatories were China and the eight countries that fought: Austria-Hungary, France, Germany, Italy, Japan, Russia, the United Kingdom, and the United States. Under the terms of the agreement, the ten top officials who were considered responsible for the rebellion were executed. In addition, the Chinese government was to pay reparations of 450 million taels of silver over a period

The mountains of Anhui, China, today.

of thirty-nine years. The U.S. used its share of the reparations to pay for scholarships for Chinese students to study in the United States. The Chinese government also agreed to educational reforms and to the long-term stationing of foreign forces in China.

Not surprisingly, the Boxer Rebellion resulted in increased foreign influence in China, not less.

The glory days of China's dynastic rule began to fade.

On February 22, 1902, the day of the Yuan Hsiao Festival, the Lantern Festival, which always fell on the fifteenth day of the First Moon, a baby boy was born in Anhui. His name was K'uei-yuan Huang. He would later be called Quentin.

1903, Anhui, China: Quentin

K'uei-yuan Huang was born into a family that, although not affluent, was comfortable. His father was an educated Confucian scholar with two Chu-Jen degrees (the equivalent of master's degrees) in military arts and literature. He worked as a farmer but also owned a restaurant. He was relentless in his assistance to the poor, earning himself the nickname "The Justice Huang."

Several weeks before K'uei-yuan's first birthday, his mother was preparing for the Chinese New Year, became ill, and died. His father, unable to care for the infant, sent K'uei-yuan to be raised by a family named Yang.

The Yang family worshipped both Buddhist and Taoist deities in their home. A large central hall in the home with a family ancestral tablet served as their gathering place. K'uei-yuan was raised as a devout Buddhist and Taoist as well as a believer in filial piety and ancestral worship as practiced by the Chinese for centuries.

1904, Niles, Michigan: Janet

The period after the Civil War saw significant expansion and growth of the Episcopal Church in America. As the country experienced urbanization and westward expansion, new churches and parishes were established in new cities and regions. Missionary work both domestically and internationally increased with the church sending missionaries to various parts of the country.

One such person was Charles John DeCoux.

DeCoux was born in Canada in 1867 to Walter and Mary DeCoux. The family came to America around 1885, and within a few years, Charles, now a reverend, was traveling the country as a missionary.

The early 1890s found DeCoux in Eau Claire, Wisconsin, where he met and married Berta Wright.

By 1899, he was head of Trinity Cathedral Grammar School in Mattoon, Illinois, which was part of the Springfield Diocese of the Episcopal Church. The family had three children in Mattoon, but they left after just a few years.

By the turn of the century, Reverend DeCoux and his family were in Michigan. There, the family had several more children.

The last was a girl named Janet, born in 1904.

1908, Gibsonia, Pennsylvania: Janet

Gibsonia lies just 17 miles from Pittsburgh and only 10 miles from the boroughs ringing the city. But in the early 1900s, these were not easy miles. The terrain in western Pennsylvania is marked with streams, ravines, hillsides, and cliffs. In 1855, Gibsonia was connected to Butler in the north and to Pittsburgh in the south by the Butler Plank Road, a venture started in part by two Gibsonia settlers, William Dickey and Richard Morrow. The road consisted of a base of crushed flag stone covered with hand-split logs. In some spots, slabs of iron and spikes were used to secure the planks. The ride was akin to riding on a washboard. Even the slowest speeds were bone jarring.

In the early 1900s, Charles Gibson, Jr., and several other investors formed the Pittsburgh and Butler Street Car Company to build a line to connect Butler, a city 33 miles north of Pittsburgh, to Etna, a borough on the Northeast side of Pittsburgh just up the Alleghany River. Once in Etna, a traveler could take any number of lines throughout Pittsburgh.

The line was operational by 1907 and had seven stops in Gibsonia. One of which was near the intersection of Dickey Road and Meridian Road. This new line made it much easier for people to travel into the growing steel city.

In 1908, a family stepped off the trolley to begin a new life. The family purchased an old farmhouse complete with a barn. The father's business would not be raising crops or livestock. It would be preaching. The new residents were Reverend Charles John DeCoux and his family, including little Janet.

The Butler Short Line passing over Dickey Road in Gibsonia, Pennsylvania. The DeCoux family stepped off the trolley and into their life in Gibsonia near this intersection. (*Photo courtesy of the Richland Township Historical Society*)

1909–1913, Anhui, China: Quentin

Anhui, China, was a complicated place in 1912. The Xinhai Revolution, also known as the Chinese Revolution of 1911, was reshaping the region. The Qing Dynasty, the last imperial dynasty of China, had been overthrown, and a new republican form of government was taking shape. Traditional Confucian values and practices which had been deeply engrained in Chinese society for centuries were challenged and replaced. During this time, foreign influence grew as the United States, Japan, and European nations sought to advance their economic and political interests.

At the age of seven, K'uei-yuan was sent to the Confucian Tutoring School to be taught the five classics and the four books of Confucius. At school, the practice was to memorize the books word for word. The students practiced their penmanship and worshipped Confucius as the greatest sage and teacher of China.

Over the next few years, K'uei-yuan became extremely accomplished as both a thinker and a calligrapher. He was asked by many residents near the school to write scrolls for them to decorate their homes for religious occasions. He earned a nickname for himself, "the young genius of the district."

At the age of eleven, his biological father felt that he had no more to learn at the Confucian tutoring school and sent him to the Cathedral School operated by the American Episcopal Church in Anking. The purpose was to study English which was the fashionable thing to do at the time.

At the school, he came into contact with people from outside of China for the first time. He was also exposed to a religion from outside of China: Christianity.

His first English teacher gave him the nickname of Paul. K'uei-yuan happily and proudly used that name—Paul Huang—until the time he became a junior in high school.

1914, Pittsburgh, Pennsylvania: Eliza

The story of Pittsburgh has always been synonymous with the story of steel. This is true as evidenced by legions of immigrants who leveraged their resolute will to turn hours in the mills into homes, education for their children, and countless communities in the hills of Western Pennsylvania.

Steel also built factories and fortunes. Underlying all of this, though, is a second story, a story of innovation. Nobody better represents this than a man lost to history, Julian Kennedy.

Kennedy was born in Poland, Ohio, a small community just outside of Youngstown, Ohio, 60 miles northeast of Pittsburgh, in 1852. He was the oldest of seven children, and his father, Thomas Walker Kennedy, was a prominent construction engineer, inventor, designer, and builder of blast furnaces. Julian attended the Sheffield Scientific School in 1875, which is now a part of Yale. He went on to work for Henry G. Morse of the Morse Bridge Company and later Carnegie Brothers & Company owned by Andrew Carnegie.

By 1890, his reputation for developing new technologies, innovative procedures, and highly efficient processes allowed him to work as an independent contractor to the steel industry.

As a steel consultant, Kennedy was a driving force behind the engineering of multiple facilities in the U.S. He also helped launch the Russia steel industry with the construction of the Nikopul Providence Steel Mill in 1896. In 1907, Kennedy built the first Indian steel mill for Tata industries, earning the nickname "Father of Asian Steel." Kennedy was a major figure in the growth and success of steel in four of the world's top ten producers: India, USA, Russia, and Ukraine.

Kennedy never stopped in his pursuit of knowledge and received master's and doctorate degrees from the Stevens Institute of Technology in 1909.

The fortune he amassed from his time in the steel industry was considerable. The family was able to travel extensively, had an expansive summer home on the Eastern Seaboard, invested carefully, and enjoyed the rewards of his hard work.

His interests, however, were not only technical in nature. He used his success to support a third part of the Pittsburgh story, the advancement of human rights. In 1904, Kennedy served as the president of the Pennsylvania women's suffrage group, the Allegheny County Equal Rights Association, which was chartered by his daughter, Lucy Kennedy, a prominent twentieth-century suffragist. She later became president of the Equal Franchise Federation of Pittsburgh and the first president of the League of Women Voters.

She would marry John Miller, vice-president of Peoples First Bank and Trust Co., a predecessor of PNC Financial Services Group. She would later go on to collaborate with her sister, Eliza Kennedy Smith, to uncover Pittsburgh city government corruption,

Pittsburgh at the time of Eliza's birth.

exposing profligate spending and improper city contract awards made by Mayor Charles H. Kline. Their investigation led to Kline's indictment by a grand jury on forty-eight counts of malfeasance and his subsequent conviction which resulted in a six-month prison sentence.

Lucy and John had three children. One was a remarkable combination of the character of her parents and relatives. She was born in 1914, and she was named Eliza after her aunt.

Eliza Miller embodied the innovative curiosity of her grandfather, the civic vision of her mother, and the tenacity of her aunt. She also had a passion that contributed to another story of Pittsburgh: art.

1915–1920, Anking, China: Quentin

As the calendar turned to 1915, the years became tumultuous for K'uei-yuan, now Paul. First, his biological father died. His father had remained an important part of his life despite the time that they spent apart. He financially supported K'uei-yuan throughout his school years, and upon his passing, K'uei-yuan was no longer able to pay for high school.

At the time, K'uei-yuan was attending St. Paul's Episcopal Missionary School in Anking. The school had been operating since 1884 and was part of a greater effort to provide medical services, social services, and relief work along with education and evangelization.

Fortunately, a new family of sorts stepped in K'uei-yuan's life, John Shryock and his wife, Margurite, were working as American missionaries in the area. John was born in 1890 in Philadelphia and Margurite was born in 1897 in Paducah, County Kentucky. So they were young, only twenty-five and eighteen respectively, but they provided an adoptive family influence for K'uei-yuan, although nothing was ever formalized. As part of his missionary work, John Shryock was teaching a teacher at St. Paul's. In addition to teaching English and physics, a remarkable combination, John was also the soccer coach. K'uei-yuan's love of the game blossomed, and his skills developed quickly.

Something else began to develop at the school as well—a passionate love of Christianity. K'uei-yuan spent hours in reflection and study and a deep connection with Christ was formed. He became a charter member of the first Chapter of the Brotherhood of Saint Andres at St. Paul's school.

K'uei-yuan's world view also began to grow during his time at Saint Paul's. He began to scrutinize the various international treaties that were impacting his life and the life of his fellow citizens. The inequities were startling, especially those within the treaties with the English, French, and Japanese. These treaties, along with the conduct of the citizens and the governments of those countries, were appalling.

K'uei-yuan's love of China and the Chinese people grew. He became proud, bold, and by his own admission, conceited. His love of Christianity faded, and he became decidedly anti-Christian. He became so anti-Christian that he refused to be called Paul any longer. He turned to a list of names found in the back of a *Webster's Dictionary* and began to sort through the names until finally coming upon one that struck him. He would be called Quentin.

Above left: K'uei-yuan, first Paul, now Quentin. (*Photo Courtesy of Alice Huang*)

Above right: John and Margurite Shryock, bottom row center, in a mission photo album later in life.

JOHN KNIGHT SHRYOCK, TARGET
"Sky" "Kid"
2140 Master Street, Philadelphia, Pa.
Civil Engineering.

Born April 28, 1890, at Philadelphia, Pa.
Entered Freshman Year; Central Manual Training High School; Philadelphia. Civil Engineering Society (4). Varsity Swimming Team (2) (3) (4). Swimming Team (1) (2). Varsity "P" (2); Intercollegiate Championship 220-yards Swim (2); 50-yards (4); 100-yards (4); Junior National Chambionship 500-yards Swim (2); Middle States Championship 100-yards Swim (3); Intercollegiate Record 220-yards Swim, Time 2.48.1 (2). Class Executive Committee (3); Class Record Committee (4); J. R. Mott Committee (4). Biddle Cup (2); Asher Cup (2); Kistler and Kerr Trophies for Swimming (3). Christian Association (4).

John Shryock as a young man.

1921–1924, Shanghai, China: Quentin

As his high school years were coming to an end, Quentin became obsessed with the idea of winning a scholarship to St. John's University, a missionary school in Shanghai. A single scholarship was given each year to the number one student of the graduating class at Saint Paul's. As an orphan, the opportunity to receive full tuition as well as room and board for four years was nearly unfathomable. It was an extraordinary award because St. John's University was regarded as the university of the rich and talented, similar to Harvard or Yale.

Quentin's determination paid off. He won the scholarship.

While at St John's University, he was not only deeply dedicated to his studies, but he also exceled athletically. He was the captain of the varsity soccer team and president of the university athletic association. He also held the rank of "All Captain" for all varsity sports. He was paired with K. C. Tung, and together they captured the doubles tennis championship of East China.

As a sophomore, Quentin was chosen to be a member of a semi-pro soccer team called Lo-Chun. Although the pay was meager, his scholarship allowed him to save nearly all of the money. He would put that to use later.

Despite all of his success in athletics, Quentin felt something missing. John and Margurite Shryock, who had remained a presence in his life, encouraged Quentin to study philosophy. He read Kant and others, and he also began to reflect on the many missionaries that worked in the community. He was moved by their Christ-like example of giving all that they had to help the members of their community, especially the children. He was also struck by the tenacity that they showed in raising money in their home countries and using it to help the truly destitute in China. These people not only preached the lessons of the Gospel, they lived them.

By the time of his college graduation from St. John's, he was once again resolute in his Christian faith. Although he no longer felt worthy of resuming the use of the name Paul, he was certain about his future. Inspired by the Shryocks, he decided that the Christian ministry would be his profession and that he would save China through service and faith.

1924–1927, Pittsburgh, Pennsylvania: Janet

On a Saturday morning in the spring of 1924, twenty-year-old Janet took a short walk along Dickey Road in Gibsonia and hopped aboard the Butler Short Line trolley. The fare was 32 cents, an appreciable amount of money then (about $5.50 today). Each car could accommodate fifty-two passengers, and the trolley traveled up to an astonishing 60 miles per hour. In less than an hour, she was in downtown Pittsburgh.

Once in downtown, Janet transferred cars to Pittsburgh's Oakland neighborhood and walked into the doors of Carnegie Tech.

The school was the product of Andrew Carnegie's generosity. Carnegie emigrated from Scotland in 1848, settled in Pittsburgh, and ultimately founded what would be the world's largest steel company by the end of the nineteenth century. In 1900, he donated $1 million for the creation of a technical institute. He envisioned a school where working-class men and women could learn practical skills, trades, and crafts. The school soon grew to offer two- and three-year certificates in the arts and engineering disciplines.

Today the school is the world-renowned Carnegie Mellon University. It is known for pioneering work in computer science, machine learning, and robotics. The school also has a highly regarded business program and is the home to the first drama program in the United States. Also, of equal if not greater importance, Dr. Scott E. Fahlman of Carnegie Mellon is credited with the invention of the smiley face emoticon :-).

The purpose of Janet's visit was the arts, specifically sculpting.

That day served as her first exposure to Joseph Bailey Ellis, a prominent instructor at Carnegie Tech.

No one knows what Janet thought upon first meeting Bailey, but his thoughts were captured in a later article. He described Janet as "... a young girl from Gibsonia who so earnestly desired an understanding and skill in this oldest branch of the fine arts that it was evident even in this first meeting that intelligence, seriousness of purpose, and quiet determination would mark her work in her chosen profession."

Janet soon enrolled full-time and studied with Bailey until 1927. Feeling that bigger creative challenges awaited her, she left for New York.

The construction of Carnegie Tech in 1912.

1925–1928, Philadelphia, Pennsylvania: Quentin

In 1740, Benjamin Franklin and several other prominent Philadelphia residents founded a charity school. In less than fifteen years, it became an academy, then a college, and after adding a medical school, it became a university. It is known today as the University of Pennsylvania.

In 1925, it welcomed an adventurous young student: Quentin Huang. John and Margurite Shryock used their connections and worked diligently to secure him a place at the school. Quentin's journey to the school covered more than 7,000 miles across the Pacific, and then the continental United States.

For the next two years, he studied intently and was also exposed to the ideals of American freedom. He was in Philadelphia, after all. He received a Master of Arts degree and then began studying at the Philadelphia Divinity School.

The school was founded by Alonzo Potter, bishop of Pennsylvania, in 1857 to educate Episcopalian priests. It was one of the first seminaries of the Episcopal Church to admit and house students of African American descent and the first to train women for service in the ministry. (Its buildings still exist as part of the University of Pennsylvania campus, but the school was closed and combined with its sister institution in Cambridge, Massachusetts, in 1974.)

While at the school, he became friends with William Thomas and a tight knit group of young men studying for the priesthood. This group would be part of a decade's long trail of notes and letters that spanned the globe.

Quentin earned degrees in 1927 and 1928. He finished all of the requirements for a doctorate but never had the opportunity to sit for his examinations. (He would later be awarded an honorary D.D. in 1942.)

In total, he earned four degrees, one at the summa cum laude level.

1927–1930, New York City: Janet

In 1927, New York City was home to nearly 12 million people. Pittsburgh, by comparison, was 600,000. Gibsonia? Barely 1,000.

Janet traveled to New York with only a suitcase, a passion for her work, and an indomitable spirit.

Using the connections of Joseph Bailey Ellis, her instructor at Carnegie Tech, she was able to find a patron in Whitney Warren, one of the founders of the Beaux's Arts Institute of Design.

Warren began practicing as an architect in New York City in 1894. One of his first clients was a lawyer named Charles Wetmore. The collaboration was so successful that Warren convinced him to become his business partner. Warren served as the principal architect, and Wetmore ran the business operations.

The firm was responsible for the design of the Grand Central Terminal in New York, but it was most well known for its hotels, including New York's Biltmore. Warren, however, took the most pride in his design of the library building of the Catholic University of Leuven in Belgium, which was finished in 1928. (The library was severely damaged by British and German forces during World War II but was completely restored after the war.)

Warren arranged a meeting for Janet with sculptor C. Paul Jennewein, who was then working on the figures for the pediment of Philadelphia's new Museum of Art. Jennewein made it clear he had little use or respect for women in the studio and instead preferred someone who could use a hammer and saw.

His demeanor was not unexpected, perhaps. Jennewein was born in 1890 in Stuttgart, Germany. His father was a die engraver and often allowed his young son to watch. Jennewein did not like school and dropped out at thirteen to become an apprentice at the Kunstmuseum in Stuttgart. He came to America in 1907 and was an apprentice at Buhler and Lauter, a New York City firm specializing in architectural sculpture. Within four years, he was on his own and secured a commission to create the ornamental sculptures for the Fifth Avenue home of John D. Rockefeller.

His next few years feel like an adventure novel: He served in the National Guard on the Texas–Mexican border, traveled to Rome where he fell in love with his Italian tutor, Gina Pirra, married her, settled in New York City, and established his own studio.

Janet managed to convince him to at least witness a demonstration of her abilities. She succeeded, and Jennewein brought her onboard for fifteen months.

After her time with Jennewein, Janet embarked on an adventure of her own.

First, she studied in Rhode Island under Aristide Berto Cianfarani, himself a protégé of Italian-born sculptor Antonio Cirino. Cianfarani was most noted for his large works. Throughout his career, he created monuments and war memorials. He also created a bust of Abraham Lincoln nearly 6 feet tall for an Italian competition and later assisted in the creation of the Borg Warner Trophy for the winner of the Indianapolis 500. It was first awarded in 1936 by then-owner of the speedway, World War I flying ace Eddie Rickenbacker.

Janet then headed west to Chicago where she spent time working with Alvin Mayer.

From Chicago, it was back to New York where her next mentor was Gozo Kawamura. He was born in Nagano, Japan, in 1884, and came to America and settled in New York in 1906. He invented an enlarging machine that helped construct significant monumental sculptures in the U.S., including the statue *The Contemplation of Justice* at the U.S. Supreme Court and several major public works in New York City. He went to create busts of President Calvin Coolidge, General Douglas MacCarthur, and others.

After her time with Kawamura, Janet worked with James Earle Fraser. As a child, Fraser began carving figures from pieces of limestone scavenged from a stone quarry close to his home near Mitchell, South Dakota. He attended classes at the School of the Art Institute of Chicago in 1890 and studied at the École des Beaux Arts and the Académie Julian in Paris in the late nineteenth century.

While serving her apprenticeships, Janet attended night school at the New York School of Industrial Arts, and the Rhode Island School of Design.

With her foundation in sculpting firmly in place, Janet traveled again.

This time, back to Pittsburgh.

Above left: Whitney Warren (1864–1943) founded Warren and Wetmore with Charles Delevan Wetmore. The firm would become one of the most prolific and successful architectural practices in the U.S.

Above right: The World War I monument in Memorial Square, Providence, Rhode Island. The work is credited to C. Paul Jennewein and Janet DeCoux is listed as a contributor.

1928, Nanchang, Kiangsi, Central China: Quentin

In 1928, Quentin returned to China and was ordained a deacon. He taught numerous classes at different schools and universities, and he also passed along his love of sports coaching soccer and tennis teams.

His ability to lead and organize groups of people also blossomed, and he and several others founded the Social Welfare Association and the Pure in Heart Church.

He also found another love, Grace Betty Song.

Grace Betty Song was born in Hsucheng, Anhei, China, in 1903. Her grandfather was a devout Buddhist general and was made a "lord" by the emperor of the Ching Dynasty for suppressing the rebellion in Formosa. Her father was an ardent Confucian scholar. Grace Betty graduated from St. Agnes' School in Anking and from Saint Mary's Hall in Shanghai. She then taught at Saint Hilda's School, Wuchang, until 1927 when she became one of the co-founders of the Social Welfare Association in Nanchang.

At the time of their courtship, her family had accumulated large land holdings in the Kiangsi province. Her father appreciated the practical work of Christian missionaries and allowed several of his children to become Christian instead of remaining Buddhist. On October 20, 1928, Quentin and Grace were married.

For the next ten years, they worked in Nanchang. Those were truly golden days in China. Quentin could see rapid advancement in almost every aspect of society and the economy, even as his own schedule became increasingly hectic. In addition to his roles at the church and welfare association, he continued his own interest in athletics, winning several tennis championships in the Kiangsi province and Central China. He was also an advisor to the athletic department of the Kiangsi provincial government. And, as an added activity, he was a correspondent for the *North China Daily News*.

Grace Betty was also busy. She was the founder and chairman of the Nanchang Mother's Club, chairman of the diocesan woman's missionary service league of the Anking diocese, a delegate to the first national woman's conference in Kuling, an organizer and promoter of children's work in Kweiyang, and a correspondent of the Kweichow daily newspaper.

During that period, Quentin was ordained to the priesthood by Reverend R. K. Huntington, bishop of Hong Kong. His family flourished. Quentin and Grace Betty welcomed Laura, Jack, Joy Ann, and Alice over the years that followed.

Sadly, Japan found the progress of China to be intimidating and invaded China in 1937.

1931, Pittsburgh, Pennsylvania: Janet

Carnegie Tech was a vibrant and rapidly evolving community in 1931. The football team, The Tartans, played as an independent team, under the leadership of seventeen-year head coach Walter Stephan. They compiled a record of 3-5-1 playing teams like Notre Dame, Purdue, Temple, Pitt, and Duquesne.

Students were forming all types of clubs from musical performance to rhetoric and debate. Students also spent time reading the campus humor magazine, *The Puppet*.

The campus was continuing to add new buildings and facilities to accommodate its growing student body, including buildings for engineering and the arts, and the school became a pioneer in exploring the properties of bituminous coal, hosting an international conference in 1931.

The school also began attracting world-class talent. As the Nazi regime began its early aggressions in Europe, many scientists sought refuge in the United States. Carnegie Tech built laboratories for Ernst Berl from the University of Darmstadt, as well as Immanuel Esterman and Otto Stern from the University of Hamburg. Albert Einstein would later visit the campus and deliver a lecture. This resulted in the only known photograph of him in front of a blackboard with a variant of his famous equation.

The school also held true to its early principles of helping the common working person. The school provided a seminar to introduce business strategies to elevator operators, bellman, and attendants taught by various people from the Pittsburgh community. The seminar was modeled after one done the previous year for waiters.

Art, too, continued to be a core part of the school, and one of their own was rewarded with an exhibit of her work: Janet DeCoux. The exhibit featured a variety of her work and drew large crowds of other students, teachers, and patrons from around town.

One visitor to the show was Eliza Miller.

1935, Europe: Janet

In 1935, Janet traveled to Europe to visit Germany, Italy, and Switzerland. Her companions were her friend Ally Moore and her husband, sculptor Bruce Moore. Each resonated with Janet for a different reason. In Ally she saw a person with a family story of triumph and tragedy as well as ferocious spirit. In Bruce she saw another artist on the cusp of well-earned recognition.

Ally's grandfather, Norman Henry Camp, was born in 1839 in Vermont. In 1861, he enlisted in the Union Army with the New York 5th Volunteer Infantry Regiment, known as the Duryee's Zouaves. Throughout the war, he rose in the ranks from corporal to major. He was cited for bravery at two different battles, including Antietam, widely considered one of the key turning points of the war. In between his engagements on the battlefield, he married Emma Winn in Rhode Island in 1864.

After the war, Ally's grandfather worked in the brokerage business on Wall Street in New York City, and then moved his family to Washington, D.C. The family had four children between 1868 and 1879, including the only daughter, Ethel, Ally's mother, born in 1874.

In 1883, he was appointed to the office of the assayer, U.S. Mint, at Boise, ID, but his western adventure soon lost its luster. In April 1885, his office was found to be missing more than $12,000, and he was arrested and charged with embezzlement. He was convicted in 1885, and the conviction was upheld on appeal in 1886. He spent the next few years in Territorial Prison (Idaho did not become a state until 1890) until he was pardoned by President Grover Cleveland.

Ethel, Ally's mother, shared her father's sense of adventure and tenacity. She did something that at the time was almost unheard of—she became a newspaper columnist.

Ethel travelled extensively writing for *The New York Times*, *The Washington Times*, and other publications. She met Emil Hugli of Berne, Switzerland, a lawyer connected with the Swiss government, in D.C. Ethel and Emil married in 1901 at the historic Saint Paul's Episcopal Church in Washington. The couple had a brief honeymoon in Italy and then settled in Switzerland. Ally (given name Alice) was born later that year. Ethel continued to work as a journalist and columnist after Ally was born using the name Ethel Hugli Camp.

Bruce Moore was born in Bern, Kansas, in 1905. (Did you catch the odd parallel? Ally's father was from Berne, Switzerland.) He showed incredible artistic promise during his youth and attended the Pennsylvania Academy of Arts studying under Albert Laessle and Charles Grafly. He briefly taught sculpture at the Municipal University of Wichita (now Wichita State University) before receiving a fellowship in 1929 from the John Simon Guggenheim Memorial Foundation to study and practice sculpture in Paris, France. His fellowship was renewed, and he met Ally. They were married in April 1931 and moved back to Kansas. Their time in Kansas was short, and they moved to Connecticut where Bruce worked as an assistant to James Earle Fraser. In 1934, he left Fraser's studio to work on his own sculptures. During this time, he created the pelican and fish for the Sloan Memorial Fountain, which earned him the Ellen P. Speyer Memorial Prize from the National Academy of Design, and the L. W. Clapp Memorial's St. Francis statue, for which he won the Helen Foster Barnett Prize also from the National Academy of Design. In 1934, he struck out on his own, and in 1935, they traveled with Janet.

As Janet was returning to America in the fall of 1935 after her trip with Ally and Bruce, she met the most interesting man on the ship; his name was Shirley. Yes, Shirley.

The Reverend Shirley Carter Hughson was born in Camden, South Carolina, in 1867 to John Scott Hughson and Eliza Randolph Turner. His father was a Confederate Civil War veteran and later became a doctor. Father Hughson received a Doctor of Divinity degree in 1919—and then became a newspaper reporter in Charleston. He then attended Johns Hopkins in Baltimore, and the General Theological Seminary in New York where he received a degree in 1896.

He eventually became renowned as an author, retreat conductor, and missioner—most notably in England.

Was he on a mission in England, or was it some newspaper connection to Alice's father that led him to being on the boat with Janet in 1935? Regardless of the connection, Father Hughson remained an important spiritual influence for Janet throughout her life.

1937, Peru, South America: Eliza

The consulting firm that Julian Kennedy founded in 1890 with Axel Sahlin, a Swedish-born engineer, grew to include a network that stretched around the globe. In addition to Kennedy's own accomplishments in Russia and India, he and his associates were influential in the iron and steel industries on six continents.

Kennedy's firm had offices in Pittsburgh and Brussels, and as time passed, they joined with a small group of engineering outfits in Britain. Later they became associated with the machine building departments of some of Germany's leading coal and steel companies.

Stories of travel across the world were prevalent in the family, and they shaped Eliza. In 1937, at the age of just twenty-three, Eliza and fellow artist Ruth Stoller headed for South America.

Her first stop was Lima, Peru. Why Lima? Her cousin, Juliann Kennedy III, worked there as an engineer for, not surprisingly, the steel industry. The timing is uncertain. Did Eliza lead him there, or did she follow Julian?

In either case, the decision to go to Lima was an adventurous one.

Lima had a tumultuous past which made it a fascinating and architecturally significant place for Eliza to visit. In pre-Columbian times, the area was first controlled by the Ichma culture and later the Incan Empire. Francisco Pizarro arrived in 1532 and ambushed the Incan ruler Atahualpa. His first choice for the capital city was Jauja, located high in the Andes, but its distance to the ocean and the altitude proved unsuitable. A Spanish scout identified a new location, the current location of the city of Lima, and the city was established in 1535.

For the next several hundred years, the city battled political unrest, disease, and earthquakes. Despite these challenging conditions, a number of remarkable buildings were created, including the Metropolitan Cathedral constructed between 1602 and 1797, the Fort of Santa Catalina built 1806–1809, and Casa de Pilatos which was constructed over hundreds of years beginning in 1590. Numerous other churches, homes, bridges, and walls were also built during this time period. All of these would have been intriguing for Eliza to study and sketch.

In 1821, the country finally won its independence from Spain. The city enjoyed some level of prosperity in the early and mid-1800s, but the War of the Pacific from 1879

Lima as it appeared at the time of Eliza's visit.

to 1893 between Chile, Bolivia, and Peru led to the destruction of critical piece of infrastructure and was the cause of the burning of the National Library.

By the early 1900s, an orderly political scene took hold, with the rivalry between the Democratic and Civilian parties. Augusto Bernardino Leguía y Salcedo of the Civilians became president, and in 1920, a new constitution was put in place. Sadly, Communism and the Great Depression fueled a new wave of political unrest. A military Junta overthrew Leguia in 1930. A political party known as APRA, who based their beliefs in a planned economy and the nationalization of industries, attempted to discredit the elections of 1931 when their candidate lost. APRA organized a series of uprisings against the military, and that enmity between APRA and the military would last for the next fifty years.

It was during this time that Eliza went to Lima and established an art studio with Ruth. They established a small studio in Lima, and from there embarked on a series of explorations that included Peru, Chile, Argentina, and Bolivia.

Eliza created an illustrated journal that chronicled her adventure.

1937, China and Japan, "The Other Start of World War II": Quentin

The "start" of World War II is engrained in the American cultural conscious with newsreel images of Japanese planes diving from the sky, torpedoes racing through the water, and American battleships burning and sinking. Sunday, December 7, 1941, the day Japan attacked the U.S. Pacific Fleet stationed at Pearl Harbor.

The results were devastating. Nineteen U.S. Navy ships were damaged or destroyed, including eight battleships. A total of 2,403 U.S. personnel were killed. Over 1,000 sailors and marines were trapped in the USS *Arizona* when it sank.

On the "day that will live in infamy," the entirety of America had already been following the war in Europe for more than two years. Back in September 1939, Hitler invaded Poland from the West. France and Britain declared war on Germany, and Soviet troops invaded Poland from the East.

After the attack on Pearl Harbor, the United States had no choice but to enter the war. Throughout the war, the Allied forces were led by "The Big Three": the United States, Great Britain, and the Soviet Union.

But the United States had another ally often forgotten: China.

China had been fighting Japan in the Second Sino-Japanese War since 1931. In September of that year, a section of railway track near the city of Mukden was destroyed by an explosion. The Japanese who owned the railway blamed Chinese nationalists. That fact was later disproven, but Japan used it as justification to retaliate and invade Manchuria.

By 1937, the tension between the two countries became untenable. A Japanese soldier deserted his post, and his commanding officer believed he was hiding in a nearby town, Beiping, in Chinese territory. The officer demanded the ability to search the town. China refused. Both sides went on alert and China fired on the Japanese troops. Ultimately, Japanese forces surged into China.

Fighting was fierce across the eastern third of China, and the front lines were demarcated in places like Kaifeng, Hsinyang, Yuehyang, and Hangchow.

One person was particularly out of place in those battles; although he would say those battles were where he was needed most: Reverend Quentin Huang.

When the war against China started in 1937, Reverend Huang was the first Christian chaplain in the Chinese army. Throughout 1937, he worked with wounded soldiers and destitute families across the front. During that time, by his count, he survived more than 265 bombings.

He referred to enduring this time as "learning real religion."

In the fall of 1937, the church pulled him from the front line and sent him to Kweiyang to organize the first Episcopal Church in the Kweichow province.

The move may have been logistical, but now it is clear evidence of Divine Providence. In December 1937, Japanese forces overran Nanjing, the capital of the Republic of China at the time. The government fled inland to Hankow, further along the Yangtze River. To break the spirit of Chinese resistance, Japanese General Matsui Iwane ordered that the city of Nanjing be destroyed. The massacre lasted for six weeks. In addition to looting and arson, Japanese forces executed over 200,000 civilians and committed more than 20,000 cases of rape.

Although Reverend Huang escaped these unspeakable acts, the war would soon find him again.

1938–1939, Gibsonia, Pennsylvania: Janet

In the 1850s and 1860s, three remarkable brothers were born into a wealthy mining family: Daniel, Solomon, and Simon. The family name was Guggenheim.

Daniel eventually became an early proponent of aviation. Solomon began collecting art in the 1890s and is best known for establishing the Solomon R. Guggenheim Foundation and the Solomon R. Guggenheim Museum in New York City. Simon was a successful businessman and was elected as a Republican to the U.S. Senate, representing Colorado from 1907 to 1913.

Sadly, Simon and his wife, Olga, lost their son at just seventeen to a rare infection. He was considered a promising young scholar and the death impacted Simon greatly.

In 1925, Simon established the Guggenheim Foundation. He wrote: "Some of the finest minds, some of the most constructive thinkers in the world, have been seriously hampered in turning their natural gifts to the best advantage by the lack of adequate financial backing. I want to do my part to meet this need."

When bestowing one of the first fellowship awards, he went on to say his goal was to "add to the education, literary, artistic, and scientific power of this country."

In the 1930s, the application process was simple, but the competition was fierce. Candidates had to provide detailed information about their achievements, submit project proposals and acquire letters of recommendation. These letters were considered crucial in establishing the applicant's merit and the significance of their proposed work.

The materials were then reviewed by a committee of experts in the relevant field and evaluated based upon the feasibility of the proposal and the potential impact of their work.

The final selections were made by the Guggenheim Foundation's Board of Trustees.

Artists, musicians, and writers used their fellowships to work in their own studios, workshops, or other creative environments where they could focus on their craft without interruption. Some worked in artist colonies such as the MacDowell Colony in New Hampshire or Yaddo in New York, which offered retreats for artists and writers.

The 1930s saw many influential figures receiving Guggenheim Fellowships, including writers like Langston Hughes and W. H. Auden, and artists like Diego Rivera.

In 1938, this renowned group of creative thinkers welcomed the newest recipient of the Guggenheim Fellowship: Janet DeCoux. "It was a joyful thing to put down someone else's tools and somebody else's plasteline [modeling clay] and somebody else's thoughts," she later wrote.

Later that year, Janet received her first paid commission from the Ursuline School of New Rochelle, New York, an institution devoted to the education of young girls. Her task was to depict the sixteenth-century founder of the order. She carved a limestone relief panel to mark the main entrance to the new library. It was considered the first "modern" building on campus.

Her work that year in totality was found to be so remarkable that she was again granted a fellowship in 1939.

1941–42, Gibsonia, Pennsylvania: Janet and Eliza

In the years that followed their brief meeting at Janet's show in 1938, the relationship between Janet and Eliza grew. Their connection through art blossomed into a lifelong companionship with the two sharing a studio space where they created art for churches, museums, collections, and public spaces around the county.

The first step in that journey took place when Eliza moved to Gibsonia to live and work with Janet. The DeCoux family home in Gibsonia was quite different from the opulent homes Eliza had experienced as a child. The oldest part of the home was a log structure that dated back to 1840 making it one of the first structures in the area. (Some documentation shows the homestead being established much earlier.) The first settler in the region was John Crawford who established his homestead just forty years before in 1800. He owned 403 acres, and his house was a simple log cabin, the gaps of which were stuffed with mud, stone, and sticks. His bed was a platform covered with oak leaves and cattails. Legend says that he slept under a bearskin blanket to stay warm.

The area was not even known by its present name until Charles Gibson helped establish the township and changed the name from Gundaker to Gibsonia in 1882.

When Eliza joined Janet on the property in 1941, over 100 years after its construction, the home was far more inviting.

Situated on nearly 10 acres, the setting included three spring-fed ponds, gardens, towering trees, and a barn, which they later converted into a studio. Over the years, they built several additions which served as both workspace and storage.

The surrounding area emerged from its agrarian roots, with small family farms with crops and livestock still dotting the landscape. The community was made up of simple schools, churches and businesses, and a blacksmith still operated nearby. Entertainment was mostly the company found in simple family gatherings, listening to phonographs, and perhaps the occasional radio program.

Things would change as America was drawn into World War II. Many young men from the area enlisted or were drafted. Eliza and Janet watched the ranks of the community dwindle, and materials for art projects were diverted to the war effort.

Perhaps it was the overwhelming stress the nation was facing, or perhaps something else moved Janet, but after completing a commission for the post office in Girard, Pennsylvania, Janet abandoned secular work. Religion had always been a large part of her life, and she increasingly sought to express her spirituality in her work. From that point on, she focused her talents solely on liturgical sculpture while looking for other ways to share her gifts and expertise.

1943, Bloomfield Hills, Michigan: Janet and Eliza

Being married to the most famous person on the planet was not always easy. Nobody knew that better than Anne Morrow Lindbergh, wife of famous aviator Charles Lindbergh, the first person to fly non-stop across the Atlantic Ocean.

In 1927, Charles Lindbergh crossed the Atlantic Ocean and became the world's most eligible bachelor. Anne was the daughter of the U.S. ambassador to Mexico, and when her father met with Lindbergh in an effort to improve the relationships with that country just seven months after that famous flight, and Anne found herself sitting beside him at dinner. By her own admission, she was tongue-tied. Lindbergh, however, appreciated her quiet contemplative nature, and the next day took the family for a ride in his airplane. She wrote in her diary: "He was so perfectly at home—all his movements mechanical. He sat easily and quietly, not rigidly, but relaxed, yet alert. One hand on the wheel—one hand! He has the most tremendous hands.... It was a complete and intense experience. I will not be happy till it happens again."

Anne did not have to wait long. After just four dates, they were engaged. Following their marriage, Anne learned how to fly and became a skilled radio operator. They flew together. They set records together. They built a family together.

Unfortunately, tragedy struck in 1932. Their twenty-month-old son, Charles Augustus Lindbergh, Jr., was kidnapped from their home on March 1 in Hopewell, New Jersey. Over the months that followed, police, government officials, government agencies, and even underworld characters attempted to find and return the baby. A series of intermediaries were used to receive ransom notes and send back offers. More than thirteen ransom notes were received.

Sadly, on May 12, the body of the kidnapped baby was found 4.5 miles from the Lindbergh home. He had been dead for two months. His skull had been crushed.

The investigation lingered for more than two years. Eventually Bruno Hauptmann was arrested and tried for the kidnapping of the baby. He was found guilty and executed in 1935.

Ann and Charles moved to Europe in 1935 to escape the hysteria surrounding the case. When World War II expanded across Europe, they returned to America. They

Anne Spencer Morrow Lindbergh (1906–2001) was most notably the wife of decorated pioneer aviator Charles Lindbergh. She was also a writer, artist, and an accomplished aviatrix in her own right.

initially supported isolationism but after the bombing of Pearl Harbor, both supported the U.S. cause.

In 1942, the family moved to the Detroit area at the invitation of Henry Ford. Charles worked as a consultant at Ford's Willow Run plant when it was converted from the production of automobiles to bombers.

Lindberg's fame was utilized as a critical component of the war effort and he spent endless months traveling selling war bonds, meeting with members of the government, and encouraging young pilots.

Anne, wanting to fill the empty hours, enrolled at the Cranbrook Academy of Art. There she studied art and sculpture. She spent many hours in class and developed an incredible bond with one of the teachers and her assistant, so much so that she invited them to live with her and help with Anne and Charles' children.

Their names? Janet DeCoux and Eliza Miller.

Those years in Cranbrook served as the foundation of a lifelong friendship marked with visits and correspondence even after Janet and Eliza returned to Gibsonia.

1944, Gibsonia: Eliza

The war years were busy for Eliza and her siblings. Her older brother, Julian Miller Kennedy, had attended Yale in 1931 and Harvard in 1936. When the war broke out, he was a member of team at the Pentagon called "Operation Grapefruit." He carried a top-secret classification, and helped evaluate information gathered from around the world. The group would distill the information into an intelligence brief that President Roosevelt reviewed at breakfast each day.

Her younger sister, Barbara, found a military man of her own. Oscar Sheffler was the son of Jewish immigrants from Romania. As a boy, his favorite memory was seeing Satchel Paige pitch in a game for the Pittsburgh Crawfords in the Negro League. He graduated from the University of Pittsburgh in 1941 and joined the army.

He was assigned to an army program at the University of Michigan, where he studied Japanese, and eventually became a translator who worked with cryptographers to crack Axis codes.

After World War II, he lived in Arlington, Virginia, and continued working as a translator for the National Security Agency.

Barbara and Oscar married in 1944, and went on to have five children: Alex, Eliza, Laura, Michael, and Peter.

The family eventually made the Pittsburgh area their home.

1938–1946, The Forgotten Theater of World War II, the Burma Road: Quentin

As battles raged in Europe and across the Pacific, China was determined to fight Japan by attacking its western flank, but Japan had choked off all of China's major supply lines and had blockaded all of China's sea ports. The U.S., China, and other Allies created and protected a narrow corridor into China stretching from eastern Burma, now Myanmar, to Kunming in the Yunnan province of China.

While U.S. supply planes would fly over the Himalayan foothills, a route called "Flying the Hump," a road was created to help expedite the delivery of munitions, food, and medicine. This was the Burma Road.

For nineteen months, legions of men, women, and children from local villages cut the 700-mile Burma Road through some of the most unforgiving land on earth. Over 2,000 road builders died. Three souls for each single mile.

Some historians call the Burma Road the greatest engineering feet of World War II.

The majesty of the road, however, was undermined with contradictions. The latest ten-wheeled American trucks shared the road with pack trains of mules and ponies. The well-supplied Allied troops traveled in vehicles while porters carried immense loads on their backs. And, maybe not surprisingly, altruism, patriotism, and selflessness were mirrored with greed, graft, and corruption. A few thousand local truck drivers, merchants, bankers, and bureaucrats carried on racketeering at an industrial scale. War supplies were literally dumped from privately owned trucks to make room for contraband goods. In some cases, the goods were hidden, while in others they were not because customs officers were in on the scheme. Trucks carrying illegal goods were given priority at checkpoints, while honest cargo was forced to wait for days. Truck drivers often used American-supplied trucks until they could swindle enough cash to buy trucks of their own.

The entire route was fraught with gangs, danger, and even Japanese bombs. American troops were targeted by surprise. The constant threat of Japanese air raids kept the level of fear and tension unnervingly high. Along the route, however, some spots of respite could be found. In the city of Kweiyang, south of the wartime capital of China, Chunking, a church was located, The Church of the Savior, founded by and led by Reverend Quentin Huang.

From 1939 to 1946, Huang often met with U.S. Army troops and American pilots. He was given the nickname the "Bishop of Burma Road." (Several grades above his true rank he would joke to the GIs.) Grace Betty was known as "Chinese Mom." So many soldiers were homesick and lonely that she started a movement for the church and private homes to be opened for meals and conversation. She also felt this would let soldiers learn Chinese culture.

During this time, Quentin also served as archdeacon of the Yun-Kwei Missionary district focusing on youth work in China. Huang established eleven chapters of the Brotherhood of St. Andre. The Church and Quentin were busy; in total, seven churches with a communicant list of 1,500 were created. Two primary schools with 567 students were established along with two kindergartens. Two hospitals, one school for blind children, and one orphanage were also founded.

Huang's work also extended to academic pursuits. In the chaos of war, a number of colleges had moved their operations from Japanese occupied areas. Huang was asked to serve as the head of the Department of Philosophy of Great China University and head of the Department of Foreign Languages and Kweiyang Teachers College.

His years of selfless giving would not go unnoticed.

Workers constructing the Burma Road.

Many portions of the Burma Road were carved from nearly vertical cliff faces.

A village along the Burma Road. An open trench serves as the sewer.

The Huang family *circa* 1944. (*Photo Courtesy of Alice Huang*)

The Huang children *circa* 1945. (*Photo Courtesy of Alice Huang*)

1946, China to Montecito, California: Quentin

In the summer of 1946, the Huang family embarked on a great adventure, they traveled along the Yangtze River to Shanghai. With their oldest child at school, it was decided that the middle two would remain in Shanghai with relatives, and Alice, the youngest, would accompany them to their final destination: America. It was not an easy trip. Alice remembers becoming extremely seasick on the Yangtze.

The reason for this visit to America was an affirmation of Quentin's accomplishments: he was to be the first bishop elected by a foreign branch of the Anglican Church to be consecrated by the church in the U.S.

On August 14, 1946, Reverend Huang was consecrated in All Saints-by-the-Sea Church in Montecito, California, with Bishop Stevens of Los Angeles serving as the chief consecrator. The "Bishop of the Burma Road" was now Bishop Quentin K. Y. Huang, bishop of Chung Hua Sheng Kung Hui, the Holy Church in China.

At his consecration, the new bishop offered a perspective that was formed by his first-hand view of the war, poverty, and political unrest he had witnessed.

> Many patriots who are strong defenders of democracy, willing to do everything possible to build a strong democracy, pay no attention whatsoever to religion or their faith, the real foundation of democracy.... We cannot love our neighbors as ourselves, if not through Christ. We cannot regard all people as equal if we do not see them as children of God.... So we cannot build a strong democracy by detaching it from its religious foundation, its motivating ideology and its soul.

Grace and Alice (left) with the Bishop (center) after his consecration with their hosts in California. (*Photo Courtesy of Alice Huang*)

Quentin at the time of his ordination. (*Photo Courtesy of Alice Huang*)

Huang was given the role of serving as the bishop of Yunkwei in the Chinese branch of Anglican Communion. His diocese would include the provinces of Yunnan in the west and Kweichow in the east.

His assessment of the area was bleak, and he pleaded for help from the U.S. church. "Starvation is rampant. People eat grass, flowers and fish bones. Medical facilities are lacking. Every phase of the Church's work is in danger of extinction through lack of funds. There are hardly three feet of level ground, three continuous days of sunshine, or three ounces of silver in the entire area."

His goals were ambitious. The list started with a plan to open more churches. There were more than 150 *hseins* (counties) in his provinces needing churches. He wanted to establish three primary schools in five years and establish another hospital in Kweiyang where land and buildings had already been acquired. He also wanted to assume the operations of a middle school where an agreement had already been reached provided that funding could be acquired.

His plea began to deliver small rewards. The American Church redirected a budget allocation listed as "Central Office, General Subsidy—$5,000" to the Yunkwei district. A second-line item of $15,000 was also created and approved. A number of other bishops also asked the consideration of the National Council in the use of monies from the Reconstruction and Advance Fund to assist Bishop Huang in his urgently needed construction program.

Bishops Huang's persistence, determination, and networking paid off. As the date of their return to China approached, they were still undercapitalized, but at least they had a small working fund.

1947–1949, America: Quentin

The new bishop's responsibilities in China were going to be enormous. His plan was to base himself and his family in Yunnan in the city of Kunming. That portion of his diocese alone covered more than 245,000 square miles in the mountainous areas surrounding Kunming. The population was astounding as well—24 million.

Before returning to the task in China, he took a lesson from the missionaries that he had admired as a youth and began an ambitious fundraising tour across America. The bishop, his wife, Grace Betty, and their youngest daughter, Alice, embarked on a tour across the country where the bishop spoke as often as possible to any audience that could be arranged.

Bishop Huang was unequivocal in his description of his homeland, "China is morally sick, spiritually sick, and physically sick."

He often spoke of the American GI's that were a part of his life on the Burma Road and was always quick to thank the U.S. for its role in World War II and stopping the Japanese threat to China. In tribute to the sacrifices of the American soldiers, the Episcopal cathedral in his district was going to be renamed the Allied War Memorial Church.

He toured thirty-eight states as part of his fundraising effort, and he leveraged his Pennsylvania connections extensively. He recruited a retired doctor, Dr. Brown, from the Philadelphia area to accompany him, and the doctor agreed to travel to China and teach young doctors there.

Above left: Alice in front a church constructed under the auspices of Bishop Huang in Kunming. (*Photo Courtesy of Alice Huang*)

Above right: The bishop and Dr. Brown. (*Photo Courtesy of Alice Huang*)

The Huang family in 1947. (*Photo Courtesy of Alice Huang*)

He spoke in Pittsburgh on several occasions as he crisscrossed the county. Bishop Austin Pardue of Pittsburgh gave him a movie projector and money for a generator, a gift that could be used in amazing ways in a land where most people had no electricity.

Alice, in her late teens, remembers the cross-country trip vividly and still thinks of the parks of the American West and the city of San Francisco.

The speaking and fundraising tour covered more than 12,000 miles across the U.S., the Pacific Ocean, and then finally across China to Kunming.

Quentin, his wife, and their associates worked tirelessly upon returning to China. By 1949, Bishop Huang with the assistance of several other Chinese priests had organized seven churches, two primary schools, two kindergartens, two hospitals, one orphanage, and one school for the blind.

He was put in charge of the Hueitien Hospital and he lived in Kunming at a large church complex called a diocesan compound that included a church, school building, a few residences, and several other structures.

1947–1949, Pittsburgh: Janet and Eliza

In the late 1940s, the newly elected Episcopal bishop of Pittsburgh, Austin Pardue, began to reshape the spiritual landscape of the region. He began a massive rebuilding project which included recruiting new clergy. Two seminarians, John Herman and Walter Moreau, were placed under the supervision of one of the archdeacons, and they were given the task of building a new parish in the area north of Pittsburgh.

The group eventually came upon the abandoned Pine Creek Covenanter church, constructed in 1837, just 5 miles south of Janet and Eliza's home. The small building was in disarray, but it became a home for the first Episcopal Mission in the northern suburbs of Pittsburgh.

The new facility was called the Pine Creek Episcopal Mission, and it took a year to make the building ready for services.

Two of the parishioners, Janet and Eliza, threw themselves into the project.

In addition to providing fellowship and labor, Janet and Eliza brought their artistic talents. The baptismal font was crafted by Eliza and a simple walnut cross was made by Janet.

Also, Marion Simpson, Janet's sister, and her husband, Paul, were early contributors.

Eliza approached the project with her usual whimsy. "Don't plan every single detail of a project, leave some room for the Holy Spirit to shape it as he sees fit."

On August 1, 1949, seminarian Walter Moreau presided over the first service and led Morning Prayer from the 1928 Book of Common Prayer. Later that year, on October 16, 1949, Bishop Pardue consecrated the church with 180 people in attendance.

Fall 1949, Kunming, Yunnan, China, Diocese Headquarters: Quentin

In the fall of 1949, Communist forces swept through China from the east to the west. The Kweichow offices of the dioceses in the east were soon cut off. For more than two months, the bishop heard nothing from his staff there and did not know whether they were in prison, or even alive.

Rumors spread that the first action of the Communists would be to decentralize all Church organizations, isolate local religious leaders, forbid the use of English, and to stop the flow of all funding from abroad.

In late November, Bishop Huang and his Diocesan Committee made the decision to set up proxy offices for Kweichow in Hong Kong, a British Colony.

One member of the committee suggested that the bishop's wife, Grace Betty, lead the effort in Hong Kong. Initially, she refused: "Many times in the Second War my husband and I were separated. This time we will remain together for better or worse. Please get someone else."

Several days later, she relented: "I guess I have to listen to God rather than my own wish, but this is the last service and there is to be no more separation in any emergency."

December 3, 1949, Kunming, Yunnan, China, Ticket Office: Quentin

While Grace Betty packed, Bishop Huang went to the ticket office to secure passage for his wife and their daughter, Alice. The bishop felt some comfort knowing that his other children were out of the country. Laura was twenty-nine and already living abroad. John and Margurite Shryock arranged for Jack to go to the University of Pennsylvania, and Bishop Thomas, the long-time friend of Quentin, secured a place for Joy Ann to go to Carnegie Tech.

As for the rest of his family, his plan was to fly Grace Betty and Alice out of the country on December 4. No flights were available. He asked about December 6. Again, no flights were available, and the prospects beyond that were dim. As he stood considering his options—none, really—two men canceled their trip on the 6th. The bishop eagerly claimed their spots for his family. The timing was more than lucky.

December 9, 1949, Yunnan, China: Quentin

Just days after Bishop Huang put his wife and daughter on a plane out of the area, Lu Han, the governor of Yunnan, surrendered himself to the Communist regime and the entire territory succumbed to Communist control.

The first step of the Communist Party to dismantle society was to pit people and groups against each other. In towns across the region, "secret reporting" boxes were installed in city squares. The message was simple: submit three names of people who you believe may be threats to the Communist government before someone submits your name.

The bishop initially dodged the impact of the reporting boxes, but on three separate occasions, he received letters denouncing him as a "running dog" of American Imperialism. The letters threatened him with death and imprisonment. With his conscious clear, and steadied by his faith, he ignored them.

At the same time, multiple plots were being executed against the bishop, solely due to the fact that he was a religious leader. Even though none of these charges gained any traction, the local Communist authorities were not going to stop targeting Bishop Huang.

Late December 1949, Yunnan, China: Quentin

The Hueitien Hospital was considered one of the best and largest medical facilities in Southwest China. It had 130 beds, twenty doctors, and forty nurses. It was originally started by the Church Missionary Society, but by the time that Bishop Huang assumed responsibility, it was treated as a secular enterprise by the hospital authorities.

This power struggle between the administration and the church, allowed for rampant infiltration by Communist Party members. In order to inflame the situation, the Communists, who were working as attendants, students, nurses, and doctors, began demanding higher salaries, better food, and different living quarters.

One week after the surrender of Lu Han, governor of Yunnan to the Communists, a man by the name of Dr. Fu, was made head of the Medical Association in Kunming by the Communist authorities. He set his sights on the hospital and Bishop Huang.

By late December, the authorities had contrived two more plots against Bishop Huang. The first involved the purchase of large amounts of yarn. As the country was collapsing and the value of the currency was plunging, the hospital bought a large amount of yarn, and used it as salaries for the employees. The rationale was simple: the currency was becoming worthless, but the yarn would at least hold its value. This was twisted into "Capitalist" ambitions. Second, the authorities implicated Bishop Huang and two others in a scheme to profit from five truckloads of medicine. In fact, the hospital had simply allowed another business to park the trucks in one of their facilities.

On December 29, two uniformed men entered the bishop's house and demanded to search the entire residence. Bishop Huang, with nothing to hide, allowed them access. The men entered the home, searched every closet, unfolded every piece of clothing, and read every word of every letter they could find. When they found a typewriter (a gift from Rev. Dr. Arthur Sherman of New York on Bishop Huang's speaking tour in 1947), they insisted it was a radio transmitter. They also found a photography light meter and insisted it, too, was a transmitter. The bishop explained the nature of the items to the men. Eventually, they relented. Finding nothing, they showed him his arrest warrant. They told the bishop they had found no evidence justifying the warrant and that the matter could be resolved if the bishop would speak with the police commissioner.

Knowing he had done nothing wrong, the bishop accompanied the men to the local police station. Their ploy worked. Once at the station, the bishop was put into custody. The bishop was immediately searched, and the guards confiscated everything: his glasses, fountain pen, pencil, Ronson lighter (a gift from an American GI in World War II), watch, pocketknife, notebook, wallet, belt, and shoelaces.

He was not given the opportunity to speak with anyone in authority and was placed in a bamboo cage. The makeshift cell was 6 by 8 feet. It held eighteen prisoners.

The bishop quickly learned that life in the wooden cage had been difficult for the prisoners. The men leaned against each other during the day and had been sleeping in a tangled pile at night. The Communist regime provided no food or water. The only chance of survival was to bribe the guards to contact a friend or relative on the outside and then bribe the guards again when any food was brought in. The political situation was so volatile that any act of helping a jailed "criminal" could easily be used to bring charges against that person. The fear of joining the men in the cage was so terrifying that few on the outside were willing to help.

Trips to the bathroom also had to be negotiated through bribery. Many could not arrange the trips, and the cage became a latrine itself. It was filthy and foul smelling with lice, fleas, and rats.

After several hours in the cage, the bishop was presented to Judge Yeh. The conversation was bleak. The judge told the bishop: "Today I am working as a judge, but tomorrow I may be one of your companions in the cage." He went on to tell the bishop that his orders were to arrest at least twenty political prisoners or suspected persons.

The bishop was astounded. He knew he had done nothing wrong.

The judge informed the bishop that his only hope was to pull some strings. The bishop said that he had no strings to pull, no connections to anyone in the Communist Party. The judge told the bishop that there was no hope for a legitimate trial. The only trials were interrogations designed to coerce the prisoner into pleading guilty to a crime that they did not commit. The only offer the judge could make is that he would try to get the bishop moved to a district jail where the conditions were better.

When the guards brought the bishop back to the cage, to his horror he saw a young girl about twelve hanging from a tree by her bound hands. Her mother was forced to sit on the ground next to the tree while the guards beat her daughter with long bamboo sticks. Two guards would take turns striking her while demanding that the girl reveal the location of her father.

The girl said nothing and was beaten more.

In the cage, the prisoners discussed the brutal beating. The guard watching the cage remarked that they had been given orders to arrest her father. The consequences for not producing him to the local authorities would be severe. Despite the pain they inflicted on both the girl and her mother, they would not divulge his location.

The girl and her mother were later brought to an area just outside the wooden cage and dropped on the muddy, filthy floor.

Later that night, three additional prisoners were brought into the cage almost lifeless. The bishop discovered that they were carpenters. They had been given a small job inside the mansion of the provincial government. Several days later, the mansion was robbed, and with no other suspects, the suspicion turned toward the carpenters. They were threatened, and then beaten with clubs, but they were steadfast in their innocence.

The three were then subjected to a device called "Tien Hua Chia." The crude device had a battery and a crank along with two wires that were attached to various parts of the prisoner. When the crank was turned, a powerful electric shock was applied to the prisoner. The men suffered hours of electrocutions before a confession was forced from them.

The bishop helped tend to the men that night.

This would be the first of seventy-nine days in prison.

January–March 1950, Prison, Kunming, China: Quentin

Early in the bishop's captivity, a man dressed in a Communist Army uniform appeared outside of the cage. He was not hostile, but very measured in his words. "I am brigade commander to the newly organized Communist Army and a relative of someone you know." (The bishop would never reveal the actual connection.) "All of your friends and

Church workers are very anxious about you but afraid to come themselves. I am their representative to see and help you. I am not a Christian, but we appreciate what you and your Church have been doing for Yunnan. Don't worry. Have patience for just a few days."

Buoyed by this small bit of hope, the bishop managed to survive by sharing meager bits of food and small sips of water that other prisoners had managed to acquire.

A note finally arrived from the officer: "The whole situation is not good. The present policy is to arrest, not to release. Be patient."

During the first ten days of the Communist control, beginning with the withdrawal of the Nationalist Army on December 21, over 10,000 civilians in the city of Kunming had been arrested.

After several weeks in captivity, a large group of guards appeared and presented an order on a tattered piece of yellow paper. Four prisoners were to be bound and made ready for a march. One of the four was Bishop Huang.

The four were handcuffed, and two guards with pistols were placed on either side, and a commanding officer marched behind them. They were marched through the heavily populated shopping district. The bishop knew this was intended to both humiliate them and send a message to the other citizens. The bishop was sure that somewhere in the crowd his friends and colleagues were watching, but they knew better than try to speak with the bishop or render any assistance.

The murmurs in the crowd were clear, "They are political prisoners, and they are taken to be shot."

The bishop decided that if this were true, he would be asked to be shot at the nearby Allied War Memorial Church, a memorial to the Allied troops who had died during the war. The bishop prayed, "O, God, Thou knowest I am not a political criminal. If I am to die as a martyr of faith, I beseech thee to let me die as a martyr of faith in thy house."

The small group was marched in a circuitous route so that as many people as possible could see them. They were stopped briefly in one public plaza. Before the bishop was able to consider if this was where he was to die, the marching resumed. Soon they arrived at the District Jail of Kunming.

The District Jail brought its own set of confusing circumstances. When they arrived, they were marched before the superintendent, a young man named Ming who was only twenty-five years old.

He looked at the group and immediately said, "Aren't you Bishop Huang?"

The bishop was surprised and unsure what this greeting might mean, but admitted to being Bishop Huang.

"I used to attend your lectures in Chung Hua Sheng Kung Hui. How did you get here? For what?"

The bishop explained the rather odd circumstances, to which the young man replied, "Well, never mind, we will take care of you."

The young man did what he could and assigned Bishop Huang and another Christian to one of the "better" rooms in the jail. The conditions were still dire. Their cell was 9 by 12 feet, and they shared it with up to a dozen other men. An open alley adjacent to a courtyard held a ditch which they used as a latrine.

Over the course of the following days, the bishop's wisdom and caring nature gradually revealed itself and he was given the nickname, "Old Bishop." Here, the "old" meant wise, kind, and worthy of reverence. While the nickname was meaningful, it did little to aid his circumstance. The prison was still run by the currency of bribes and favors.

One afternoon, one of Ming's assistants was checking on the prisoners and the bishop sensed he was in some discomfort. Ashamedly, the assistant admitted he was suffering from gonorrhea. The bishop realized this was an opportunity to bring some comfort to the men of the prison and made a simple offer. "Bring me sixty copies of the New Testament and I will give you a contact on the outside and a referral so you can get some medicine."

The following morning, Bishop Huang held his first bible study for the prisoners of the district jail. The classes soon expanded and after several weeks, each of the bibles were being used and sometimes shared. While the bishop took great comfort in saying the Lord's Prayer with the men, he was most touched by their personal, heartfelt prayers for their families and each other.

As more prisoners were brought into the jail, the story of what was happening outside gradually began to take shape. The "reporting boxes" were providing a constant stream of names. Aside from political motivations, people used the boxes as a form or retribution. Business partners, quarrelling neighbors, feuding family members, and people carrying all sorts of prejudices began filling the ballot boxes with names and the jails filled up as quickly.

The bishop's jail contained bank managers, newspaper editors, college professors, priests, monks, and more, most without named accusers or formal charges.

One morning in January, the bishop noticed that he was getting odd looks from other prisoners, and he heard his name mumbled in several conversations. He confronted one man, and the man informed the bishop that the Communist newspaper had run a story about the bishop outlining the charges against him: First, using his religious mission as a cover the bishop had built a network of spies in both the Yunnan and Kweichow provinces. Second, the bishop himself was working as a spy. Third, he was using funds embezzled from the hospital to send Church workers to America to be trained as spies against the government. The bishop was labeled as the "the Number One American Spy" in all of China. The bishop sank against the wall. To add further insult to the charges, the Communists had fabricated an organization and claimed that they were responsible for the charges. The fake organization had been given the name, the "Kunming Christian Fellowship."

Most in the prison realized the charges were false. Others, uncertain, began to distance themselves from the bishop.

Life for the prisoner's families began to unravel outside of the jail as well. Many had been salaried workers and shopkeepers. Their finances deteriorated rapidly while they were in jail. Their wives and family members sold possessions, but with fewer people working, almost nobody was willing to, or could in fact, afford almost anything. Children dropped out of school, and wives returned home to their parents. The Communist authorities began to bring the prisoners some food, because many who had relied on outside assistance were now starving.

The jailers would bring the cell what the prisoners called, "glass soup." It was so thin, and so lacking of any substance, that it appeared nearly clear. The only reprieve was the first and fifteenth of the month when two or three pieces of pork were added to the soup.

Food was also used to subtly begin communist indoctrination. If a family member brought you a small morsel of food, you were encouraged to share—not because it was a morally plausible thing to do, but because it was said that it reinforced the idea that you had no personal possessions. Anything that you owned truly belonged to the government and that it was theirs to redistribute.

After attending the bishop's bible classes for several weeks, the authorities informed the prisoners that they would be held in jail longer if they continued to attend the bible classes, and the jailers decreed that the only books to be read were the nine new books on communism. The books were misguidedly referred to as the "Nine New Books of Democracy." The prison was organized into twenty-seven study groups each with an administrator and secretary. It soon became apparent that these leaders could reward and punish whomever they pleased based upon that person's performance.

Rumors were purposefully spread among the prisoners that those successfully learning the nine books would be released by mid-January. At the same time, the prisoners were informed that only eighteen out of the 317 held in the jail were truly political prisoners and that most would be released provided they had read the propaganda.

This had the desired effect, and the prisoners began to study with vigor. Within days, several prisoners approached the administrator saying that they had learned the material and were willing to be tested on any of the nine books. The response made it clear that there was no test and no actual chance of release.

Despair was taking hold inside and outside of the prison.

One railroad man who had worked loyally for twelve years had been imprisoned on the recommendation from his subordinates for his "imperialism" was visited by his wife at one of the prison's windows. She passed him a note: "Our children have been selling newspapers these days but there is no sale. We have sold everything we have. There is no friend or relative from whom we may borrow as they are all poor now. The railroad union has stopped your salary as you are imprisoned. I have done my utmost. I cannot do more. Sorry for the kids. Take care of yourself. Good-bye."

Early the next morning, one of his boys came to the prison and told him that their mother committed suicide while they were asleep.

Another prisoner, about thirty years old, who had once been an officer in the National Army, had married a beautiful girl from Soochow, Kiangsu. After World War II, instead of going to Soochow, they decided to settle in Kunming. The husband became a teacher, they had a child, and they enjoyed a wonderful, loving life. Unfortunately, a few of his students, upset with his strict demeanor, submitted him as an enemy of the state. After his imprisonment, his income was stopped, their savings were soon exhausted, and they became impoverished.

He was passed a document and a small note from his wife that stated, "To relieve you from your worries and to save us from starvation, please sign this document." The man opened it to find divorce papers. A member of the party had designs on her and used starvation as a way to steal her.

Days later, the jail was placed into a lockdown. A prisoner who was formerly an administrator at the Ammunition Factory in Kunming was so distraught over his life in jail and the misery being endured by his family attempted to hang himself with a strip of sheets while his cellmates were asleep. Fortunately, the iron bars of the window where he tied the sheet were not high enough from the ground, and one of his cellmates was able to save him.

The Communists continued to press the idea of indoctrination with the false promise of freedom. They instituted a policy of writing two papers. One was a "Tzi Pei Hsu," an autobiography, and the second a "Tan Pei Hsu," a confession.

The bishop reviewed the requirements of the autobiography: your parentage, date and place of birth, education, profession, etc. Nothing too out of the ordinary. But the last requirements were sinister: the reason and date of your arrest, and lastly how you planned to redeem yourself in the eyes of the party.

The Tan Pei Hsu was worse. It required you to restate your biography and then add the place and day of your spy training, the spy work you had been assigned to do, the spies you knew along with their assignments. Lastly, if you were not a spy, you were to add a "self-conclusion." This part was to contain self-criticism, self-redemption, and self-determination.

The bishop recognized the ploy immediately: terrorize someone with the threat of being and spy, and make them feel grateful for the opportunity to criticize their life and character along with a promise to redeem oneself with a path that served the Communist state.

The jails administrators gave speeches on what a great chance of freedom this represented, and often repeated the line, "Honest confessors will be forgiven."

Of the confessions written in the jail, only a few of the 317 submitted were considered honest. These were actually written by Communist plants living among the prisoners pretending to be "justly" jailed. These bogus confessions were read repeatedly at assemblies as examples of how to write a proper confession.

Prisoners were asked to write their biography and confession multiple times. Hunger, exhaustion, and mental fatigue often led to small discrepancies in each interaction. The Communist authorities pounced on the small differences leading to hours of interrogation.

The bishop adhered to an old Christian adage: "The truth will set you free."

Frustrated by the lack of progress they were making in his indoctrination, and the lack of discrepancies in his work, the bishop only wrote his biography once and his "confession" four times. His "affiliations" were limited to knowing people in the Roman Catholic Church in China, the American Episcopal Church, and the Church of England. He provided details about working with orphans during World War II. For the most part, he and the church worked independently in China, and although they sometimes felt isolated from the greater church community, it gave him, fortunately, little foreign connections to write.

In the days that followed the writing of the biographies and confessions, the trials began. Cases of "minor infractions" were held during the day and serious trials were held at night.

The minor trials consisted of the prisoners reciting their biography and confession. Any hesitation was seen as uncertainty and an attempt at deception, so the prisoners spent hours memorizing every word of their documents. The judges would then ask the defendant questions for hours. The goal was never to find any new information, only to create an inconsistency which could be used against the prisoner. The afternoon trials as a rule lead to no conclusion or sentence. Prisoners were simply sent back to their cell.

The night trials were different, and the evenings became terrifying. The cell doors were locked at 8:30 p.m., and hours later, a prisoner would be roused with no warning, blindfolded, and marched to the trial where five judges would take turns questioning the prisoners. When the judges desired, often for no reason, the prisoner would be beaten and electrocuted. The trials lasted to the early hours of the morning, and the prisoners would often be deposited near lifeless back in his cell.

In late February, the bishop was called for his trial. Blessedly, it was an afternoon trial. The bishop was taken to the warden's living quarters and presented to a man named Judge Chen. The bishop recited his documents precisely with no stops or breaks.

The judge then began to ask the bishop a long list of questions, mostly regarding the various denominations operating in China, their leadership and their structure. Mixed with these were questions designed to agitate the bishop like, "Why does this other denomination not like you?" and "Why does this particular church have a low opinion of you?"

The bishop stated honestly that he knew nothing about the organization and leadership of the other churches. The other questions he assumed were an attempt to make him feel hostility towards other denominations and he simply pleaded ignorance to those insinuations.

As the trial came to a close, the judge asked the bishop one final question: "Do you think it is possible to organize all denominations into one church?"

The bishop, who had only had positive interaction with other denominations and had seen the good work of their charities and missionaries, said it was neither practical nor wise. The judge seemed disappointed by the response and sent the bishop back to his cell, promising that he would have a decision shortly.

Days passed, and the bishop resolved himself to the fact that no freedom was in sight. To his surprise, members from various Communist departments and agencies began visiting his cell. They began to ask him questions about various church teachings. Soon, however, the bishop realized that this was not a conversation driven by spiritual curiosity. It was an investigation tied to some plot or scheme. Oddly, throughout these conversations, they made it clear to the bishop that he was not under investigation for his religious beliefs rather his conduct at the hospital. The bishop was able to ask them a series of circuitous questions over the course of several days before finely uncovering their motivation. The new regime did not want religious organizations building goodwill with the citizens through the care provided by religiously affiliated hospitals. The Communists believed that all hospitals should be run by the state. Across the county religious leaders who staunchly defended their hospitals were imprisoned under bogus charges and many were killed.

March 1950, Prison, Kunming, China: Quentin

In early March, the bishop was called for his second trial. The bishop was informed that the judge was a senior leader of the party. The bishop began his recitation, and although the judge asked him to repeat a few parts and speak slower on occasion, he did not seem interested. When the bishop finished, the judge asked him: "Do you still believe in God."

The bishop resolutely responded, "Yes, I still believe in God and my faith has been strengthened by my time in jail."

The judge then asked the bishop about any land holdings he had or wealth that he accumulated.

The bishop replied honestly; he was "propertyless." Later the bishop discovered that two men were sent to the church compound to verify the statement. The janitor and several others all gave the same answer: "He owns but three pairs of trousers."

Again, the trial ended with no conclusion or resolution and the bishop was sent back to jail.

After the trials, and the release of no prisoners, the Communist authorities intensified their efforts at indoctrination. All of the prisoners were required to write a third paper, a "Tzi Sheng Hsu," a self-examination. In order to "help" the prisoners, they were given a book called the *Directory of Thought*, which instructed them to review their parents' lives, how they were raised, and then how the prisoners themselves were raised, and subsequently how they might change their beliefs to a new way of thinking. The goal was to make the prisoners think less of their own families and the value of a family, and make each believe that the government, in fact, was the key element of society. Not families. Not individuals.

The Communist Party made it very clear of their interest in controlling the minds, wills, and future of children. They believed children were "blank sheets of paper" which could be filled with the party narrative. They were anxious to penetrate kindergartens, primary schools, middle schools, high schools, and colleges. They wanted control of all of them. Sadly, they were especially fixated on orphanages.

After writing their self-examinations, the prisoners were brought before study groups where they were forced to read their statements. Those that attacked their forefathers, upbringing, and education were given preferential treatment, while others were interrogated for hours with endless streams of questions.

The prisoners talked tirelessly amongst themselves about how to avoid the mental torture of the interrogation. One said, "We simply need to pretend to be actors on a stage, and tell them what they want to hear."

Bishop Huang felt that he could not do so. It was not in his heart to lie about his family and the culture of past China that he believed so strongly in. When it was time for him to go before the group, he talked truthfully about his past and awaited his criticism. The group was confused by his honesty and his lack of interest in politics.

His desire to help fellow citizens simply as humans was not a stance the jailers knew how to handle.

March 12, 1950, Prison, Kunming, China: Quentin

Late in the afternoon, a guard appeared at the cell where the bishop was being kept, and his name was called again. This was his third trial, and as an afternoon trial, the bishop was concerned but not as terrified as if it had been a night trial.

He was presented to a judge who greeted him oddly, "Do you remember me?"

The bishop apologized and citing his hunger and extreme exhaustion said that he did not.

The judge said that he was a former theological student, and the reminder immediately refreshed the bishop's memory. However, in these times where some truly converted to communism and other merely acted out the role, the bishop did not know whether he could trust this judge in any way.

The judge confided that there were still three standing charges against the bishop. The first was that he was an American spy. This was justified by the time that he spent with GI's during the war, the fact that he had been consecrated in America, and the amount of correspondence he had with people in America. The second charge was that he was a spy of the Nationalist government. The third was that he used funds from the hospital to send church workers to America to be trained as spies.

The judge went on to say that the second and third charges had been investigated and were being removed. However, the first charge still stood—he was an American spy.

The bishop responded exasperated, "You know I have never been a spy and know nothing about spying. If I were accused of preaching the Gospel, I would readily admit it! But as for being a spy, I will never confess!"

The judge thought for a while, and said, "Although the charge is very serious, it can be addressed, provided that you are willing to serve the people. You understand what the New Democracy means." (The bishop did and hated every way that the Communists contorted the word Democracy.) "There is no use for Christians to talk about the life beyond. Let's us talk about life here. There is no sense to talk about and preach the Kingdom of God. Let's us build a classless Utopia."

While he was talking, the bishop could only think of the phrase, "Get thee hence Satan!"

The judge ended his twisted philosophical statement with a question, "Have you decided to serve the people? This is the only question I would like answered."

"Yes," the bishop answered. "Otherwise I would not be working in the Church."

The judge considered that answer and, deciding that it could be useful, sent the bishop back to his cell.

Upon returning to his cell, and finding his space on the mat, another prisoner who the bishop knew was a Communist agent planted among them whispered, "I am glad that you have decided to serve the people. You will be released in a few days. You will be the great leader of the religious revolution in Southwest China."

The bishop was astounded by how fast his answer had traveled through the jail, and he pressed the man, "What do you mean 'a great leader.'"

The man replied, "You will know when you get your assignment."

"Assignment?" the bishop asked, surprised. "What assignment?"

The man would offer no more details, but the bishop would not relent and continued to ply him for details.

The man realized the bishop was not going to give up and lowered his tone. "I am going to let you know, but you must keep my name very confidential. Your first assignment will be the indoctrination of all the Church Workers and Christians in Kunming. This should be easy for you. If you prove yourself faithful and loyal, you will be made head of the United Church in this area. If you like, you will be asked to take charge of all religions in this area."

March 17, 1950, Prison, Kunming, China: Quentin

After seventy-nine days in jail, the bishop was released with little fanfare. His instructions from the judge had been simple, but chilling: he was to have several days to gather his possessions at the church compound. After that he was to be in charge of the United Church in southwest China. His role was to be the leader of all religious churches and instill a doctrine that said all faiths must be subservient to the Communist Party. The choice he was given was clear: instruct all people of faith that the government must be put first and all religion second. If he failed to do so, the bishop would be sent back to jail, and then be subjected to further punishment. The bishop knew what this meant: failing to carry out his orders would mean his execution.

He was asked to provide names of two people from the Diocesan House, the church compound, who might be able to come and get him.

Was this a trick? Would they be arrested?

After a quick thought and prayer, the bishop offered two names.

Surprisingly, after just thirty minutes, the bishop was led outside and released into the waiting arms of his friends.

March 18, 1950, Kunming, China: Quentin

The bishop made his time in jail a period of prayer, reflection, and ministry. After his release, he told his friends that it was an experience he would not have traded, but the days in prison were not good for his health. He dropped 27 pounds from his already lean frame, and he was afflicted with high tone deafness. He had also developed a large mass of skin on his back, and his legs were woefully skinny.

None of these things bothered him nearly as much as the ultimatum of becoming an instrument of the Communist Party or facing the consequences.

The bishop spent the next few days in the church compound and discussed his predicament with several close friends. He would pray long into the night asking God for some direction.

A brief reprieve came from a doctor. Upon seeing the condition of the bishop, the doctor ordered one month of rest before the bishop would be allowed to assume any of his new duties. Fortunately, a member of the Communist Party working for the Ministry of Public Safety reviewed the order and approved it saying, "Have a good rest. We'll see you in one month."

The next few weeks passed quickly, and his dilemma became more troublesome even as his health improved.

He gradually came to the conclusion that he would reject the offer. He knew this would ultimately mean going back to jail. His other option? Escape.

The economy, social systems, and even the basics of transportation were in utter chaos as the Communist Party increasingly controlled every aspect of the country and people's lives. No planes, buses, or means of mass transportation were available.

Only three overland routes were plausible:

1. A highway that traveled east to Kweichow, Kwangsi, and Kwangtung.
2. A highway that traveled south to IndoChina.
3. The Burma Road that led west to Burma.

The eastern highway had been tried by others, but they had encountered a lawless land run by bandits and loose affiliations of disbanded soldiers.

The southern route was marked by battles still raging between Communist and Nationalist forces.

The Burma Road route, nearly 700 miles long, was politically stable, but only because it was completely controlled by Communist forces. Heavy garrisons had been established along the route and groups of soldiers patrolled the border constantly. However, the Communist mindset was often erratic and barbaric. People were regularly stopped and accosted for no reason by the Communist forces. Harsh interrogations and imprisonment were common with no reason or justification given. Local police forces in an attempt to win favor with the party were equally brutal, and there was little to no judicial process for the people they chose to target.

The bishop also knew that transportation was going to be a problem. The government had commandeered all private and commercial vehicles.

March 19, 1950, Kunming, China: Quentin

The bishop woke up excitedly in anticipation of a service which would advance one deacon to the priesthood and would see two others ordained as deacons.

As he prepared for the day's events, a colleague mentioned sympathetically that a young couple staying on the grounds had been married a few weeks earlier, but did not have the opportunity to have a ceremony.

The bishop recognized the ruse immediately and whispered to his friend, "spies."

Over his time in prison, the bishop became highly attuned to the Communist Party's tactics. A person who dropped unexpectedly into your life was most likely planted there to spy. When a person's demeanor did not match their circumstance or story, they were typically spying. And, sadly, people who were overly friendly or complimentary were often spying as well. In all of these cases their goal was to find some small fact or action which could be contorted into a case against you.

The couple masquerading as a young married couple was spying on everyone in the church compound, and this was proven to be true later that night.

At eleven o'clock, six soldiers pounded on the gate of the church complex. The colleague who the bishop had been talking with earlier that day was named as a person of suspicion by the soldiers. The soldiers searched the cathedral and other church buildings. When they made their way to the home where the bishop was staying, the bishop opened his door to find his young colleague flanked by a Communist Party officer. The young man was despondent and asked the bishop for his advice. The bishop could only tell him to be honest as he had done nothing wrong and to pray. The Communist officer eyed the bishop suspiciously. He found the advice of prayer to be clearly against the wishes of the party.

The soldier placed the bishop under house arrest. He was not to leave the property for any reason at any time.

March 20, 1950, Kunming, China: Quentin

The bishop's colleague reappeared after being released from prison shortly before lunch. He was allowed to go free under the promise that he would go on the radio and give a ten-minute talk to Christians on the privileges and benefits of buying bonds from the new Chinese government.

The bishop knew that this was just one example of many that he would see of the leverage that the Communist Party exerted against people. Fear of imprisonment impacted people differently. His friend had managed to tolerate only one night in jail.

That afternoon a party official arrived and informed the bishop that the hospital he had helped start would be soon placed under government control.

In order to "celebrate" the transition, they had decided to hold a "Welcome Home" party for the bishop later that week. His role in the festivities would be simple. He would simply have to give a speech declaring that his management practices were not as polished as they should have been, and that the staff should embrace the guidance from the new Communist administrators.

The bishop recoiled at the offer, deeming it a humiliation party.

The bishop was then given more instructions for his conduct and demeanor. Underlying this was the order that the bishop would begin to steer the local Christian community away from the Church.

When the party official left, the bishop considered his options. It had been made clear that he was still under house arrest. The bishop also surmised that refusing to attend the party would lead to his immediate return to prison. While he could stomach the orders regarding the hospital, the insinuation that he needed to lead people away from God was truly troubling. He reflected on the last page of the book *New Democracy* by Mao Tze-Tung. It stated that no member of the Party will be allowed to have anything to do with religion.

The bishop came to the conclusion: "No man can serve two masters. He who is not with Me is against Me. The same is true with Christianity and Communism."

He knew he had to escape. But how?

March 21, 1950, Kunming, China: Quentin

When the bishop was released nearly a week earlier, many friends and acquaintances had reached out with not only well wishes but with offers of places to stay. Remaining at the church compound offered the comfort of familiarity, but also the constant threat of spies. The bishop knew he was still under house arrest, but staying or leaving both felt likely to lead to being arrested.

He looked over the notes he had received and was drawn to an offer from a person he had known for years but rarely saw. Their professional and personal circles did not overlap, and their lives rarely crossed paths. This person, however, owned a house on the outskirts of town in an inconspicuous neighborhood. More importantly, the bishop felt he could trust him, and given all of the circumstances, the bishop was willing to gamble that the person had not succumbed to Communist pressures.

Early in the morning while everyone else in the church compound was just beginning their day with breakfast and morning chores, the bishop packed a suitcase. His belongings were meager: two pairs of socks, some underwear, two shirts, two pairs of pants and a copy of the New Testament in Chinese. He spoke to nobody, found a back gate that opened into an alley, and slipped into the city.

Violating his house arrest would be grounds to send him back to prison and he knew it.

The bishop attempted to appear casual as he walked the streets. So many people had been displaced by the war and instability that a man carrying a suitcase seemed rather normal. His age and worn-down appearance drew no suspicion from the occasional Communist guards at various intersections.

After an hour of walking, he arrived at his friend's house.

His friend, surprised but excited, showed the bishop to separate living quarters attached to the home, and he quickly settled in.

Over the next few days, the bishop established a schedule of eating, sleeping, praying, and reading the Bible. He joined the family for their meals throughout the day but spent the remainder of his time in solitude asking God to reveal a plan for him. The family kept his presence a secret, and nobody at the church compound had any idea what had happened to him.

After a week, he regained some of his strength and weight. He began to visit with his host and review his options: become an instrument of the Communist Party, refuse and go to jail, or escape.

The bishop also wondered if he could just delay the Communist instructions with a series of excuses and diversions until they finally lost interest in him. His host understood the party well and knew they would not let the bishop simply stall. He also knew that they had identified Quentin as a potential tool and would not allow him to simply fade into everyday life. His recommendation was simple: you must escape.

Quentin countered: "I am the head of our church and the shepherd of my flock. In times of distress I should stay more closely with them and not leave them to the wolves."

The host felt the odds of escaping were 50:50. Being caught meant certain imprisonment, but if Quentin stayed, he would not be allowed to be a shepherd to the flock. The Communists would concoct conspiracies and legal transgressions targeting the community, and they would use the bishop as a forced witness of stature to gain convictions. The Communists would force him to testify against his congregants.

Escaping would not mean the bishop abandoned them, but it would perhaps give them a reprieve from their own imprisonment.

March 30, 1950, The Suburbs of Kunming, China: Quentin

The bishop awoke to the sound of a quiet knock on his door. To his surprise, Quentin opened the door and found not only his host, but a lady accompanying him. His host quickly assured the bishop that she could be trusted, and more importantly she was here to offer him a means of escape. (Quentin never revealed the true identity of the woman throughout his entire life for fear that she would be subject to some form of reprisals. He only spoke of her using the codename, "Lydia.")

Lydia told Bishop Huang that she had a friend who owned three trucks, and that he had been ordered by the Communist government to go to Burma to pick up loads of cotton. The owner of the government haggled over the price of his services and the trucks, and the government finally agreed to let the trucks carry passengers for various parts of the route. The owner was free to charge what he wished and keep the fares from the passengers.

Lydia offered to allow the bishop to hide among the passengers and to use her connections to help him cross into Burma. Quentin was overjoyed by the opportunity, but a sense of fear gripped him.

He was instructed to be ready immediately.

April 2, 1950, The Suburbs of Kunming, China: Quentin

When Lydia met Quentin at his host's home, she told him that they would break the escape into two parts. First, a jeep would take them to the outskirts of town using a winding route to avoid as many checkpoints as possible. Next, they would rendezvous with the trucks and begin the long drive to Burma.

With no choice and no time to reconsider his options, Bishop Huang hurriedly agreed to the plan. Within minutes, the jeep arrived. The escape began.

The driver chose his route carefully, but they regularly saw small groups of men in Lenin uniforms marching with their pistols.

The jeep left the city and climbed to an area outside of Kunming City called the Western Hills. On one of the hairpin curves overlooking the city, the bishop paused and said: "Farewell, Kunming, May God bless you and strengthen the God-loving people in the city in their struggle against the ungodly."

At the top of the hill awaited a checkpoint. Quentin had been preparing and expected to be interrogated. When they reached the top, the guard looked at him and mistook his age and appearance as authority. He saluted the bishop and let them pass!

The group stopped at a small town 20 miles west of Kunming, where they were to meet the trucks. The driver, Quentin, and Lydia found seats at a small tea shop where they could keep an eye on the road. An hour of waiting turned into two, and then three. They watched as thousands of Chinese Communist soldiers marched in groups to Tali and Paoshan. The trio tried to remain as inconspicuous as possible, but as the day wore on, the hopes of the trucks arriving faded.

Staying in the little town was not an option. As outsiders, they would become a target for both the Communist patrols and the local bandits. Sadly, when the afternoon passed into evening, the group retraced their route to Kunming.

Back at the safe house, Quentin was informed that a messenger had been sent to tell them that the trucks were postponed for a day. One of the trucks was extorted by the government for a "road repair fee" which they had to hurriedly borrow, and a passenger had been randomly pulled from the second truck and taken to the local Communist Party office for questioning.

A new rendezvous place had been picked for early the next morning just beyond the Western Hills.

That night, the bishop debated as to whether the mounting troubles were a sign from God to stay in Kunming. Again, his friends assured him that he would have no future there—only service to the party or prison.

April 3, 1950, The Suburbs of Kunming, China: Quentin

The morning brought unseasonably cold weather. The group left at 7 a.m. and followed the same initial route as the day before. At the top of the hill outside of town, the guards refused to leave their small shack due to the cold and simply waved the group past.

At the base of the hill the jeep stopped at the rendezvous point. Lydia sat inside a small cafe, and the bishop waited outside for the trucks. He spent three hours in the cold before the trucks arrived.

Shortly before noon, Quentin spotted the first truck. It was open, the canvas cover which had once protected the back was so worn that it was simply pushed aside. He and Lydia joined thirteen adults and two children sitting on top of all of their possessions—trunks, boxes and suitcases.

The truck rolled along the highway for hours and eventually met with the other two trucks. The yellow dust from the gravel encircled the passengers, coating them in a thick layer of grime. When going up hills, every male passenger was required to get off and walk. The trucks were underpowered because they had been hastily configured to run off of alcohol because the Communist government had confiscated all of the gasoline.

At the end of the first day, the truck arrived at Chu-hsiung. A shopkeeper in Lydia's network took them in and offered them a meal and a covert place to sleep.

The next morning, the truck drivers complained that they had not nearly had enough sleep. During the night, Communist patrols had repeatedly inspected every piece of luggage on the truck and had detained the drivers, interrogating them for hours.

April 4, 1950, The Burma Road, China: Quentin

The three truck drivers decided to travel more closely together that day. The drivers believed they would be a more inconvenient group to stop and interrogate since the patrols would not want the headache of dealing with so many passengers and belongings. The strategy worked but created an incredible amount of dust. Once again, the male passengers were forced to walk up the mountains.

Just before dark, the trucks arrived at a highway crossroads outside of Hsia Kwan. The area was thick with Communist guards. The bishop was dozing and was slow to react to the order to dismount the truck. By the time he realized what was happening and jumped from the truck, the guards had moved on to the next truck.

A singular guard approached him and asked him for his name. Shocked, he simply said, "I am the Bishop of the Holy Church in Yunkwei and am a passenger going to the western part of Yunnan." This was true, of course, but the bishop left out the fact that his final destination would be a little further. The soldier, shocked by the directness and politeness of the bishop's answer, simply nodded and left him standing in the road.

The trucks were soon underway, and as night fell, they arrived in Hsia Kwan. They found the opportunity to wash and enjoy some food in a restaurant which was controlled by another of Lydia's contacts. While they were eating one of the truck drivers asked if anyone would volunteer to sleep on top of the truck that night and guard the cargo, so he could stay with his family that happened to live in the area. Quentin, feeling fortunate, agreed. While Lydia and the other passengers checked into a hotel, he climbed atop the truck, arranged a spot to sleep among the cargo, covered himself in blankets, part of the canvas top, and other items, and was soon asleep.

In the early hours of the morning, a Communist patrol raided the hotel and questioned all of the passengers for hours, including Lydia. One female passenger was told she was going to be arrested due to her unacceptable paperwork. She began to cry hysterically, and the patrol not wanting to deal with the hysterics let her remain with the group.

April 5, 1950, The Burma Road, China: Quentin

After Hsia Kwan, the Burma Road narrowed, and its condition worsened. The vehicles had to slow accordingly, and the entire day was spent traveling to the town of Paoshan in Western Yunnan. The city was the center of Communist activities for the region. A large number of Communist troops were stationed there with the orders to control Western Yunnan and the frontier between Burma and China.

The mountains outside of Kunming today.

Lydia felt that Quentin would be safer with the group and recommended he stay in the hotel with the rest of the travelers. He agreed, sensing that Lydia had a unique ability to assess the situation. That night, a Communist patrol and a police patrol conducted sweeps of the hotel. The police patrol was thorough, skipping only two rooms. One of the rooms was where the bishop hid.

April 6–8, 1950, The Burma Road, China: Quentin

For the next three days, the trucks proceeded along the Burma Road. The days were an endless cycle of fear, exhilaration, walking, sleeping on the trucks, and watching every patrol with uneasiness.

The roads and bridges were in such bad repair that the drivers would often detour around the bridges and instead choose to find a shallow spot in the river and drive through the water.

On April 8, the trucks reached the border town of Hwanting. Amazingly, they had covered the 700 miles and evaded Communist patrols, local police, and extorting bandits; they had even avoided mechanical breakdowns. But Hwanting was different from the other places they had passed through. It was a heavily patrolled border town.

Lydia could sense Quentin's apprehension and would say, "Don't worry, you will get through. For God is with you."

When the truck pulled to a stop, the bishop retrieved his Episcopal ring which he had hidden in the bottom of a jar of Vaseline and put it deep within his trouser pocket. Together with Lydia, he made the decision to cross the border at 2 p.m., when the heat and humidity would be most oppressive.

When the time came, the bishop approached the customs house on the border. He noticed that all of the soldiers, policemen, and guards were in the customs house trying to find some comfort in the shade. Only a single guard was on the road. As the bishop's stride narrowed the gap, he could see that the guard was talking to a young woman that he could only describe as beautiful.

He knew this was his opportunity. He passed the guard and stepped onto the international bridge. He never looked back. He never quickened his pace. He said a prayer.

He was free! He could see his family again!

His obligation to become a tool of the Communist Party and his orders to remain under house arrest were behind him. Well, not entirely.

He knew that attempts to contact friends in Rangoon or Hong Kong could tip the authorities as to his location. Legally he could be imprisoned in Burma and returned to China. The bishop blended into a crowd at a coffee shop at the town of Chiu Koo and debated his next move.

A young man approached and said, "How are you, Bishop? What are you doing here?"

Quentin was terrified and played dumb. "What did you say?

"You are Bishop Huang, aren't you? I was in Kunming and attended Sunday Services regularly at St. John's Cathedral."

He studied the young man and began to ask him a series of questions as casually as he could. When Quentin determined that he could be trusted, he told the young man of his plight. The young man told the bishop to remain in the coffee shop and await his return. Was this a set up? Would he be arrested?

The next hour passed slowly, and the young man finally returned. Mercifully, he was alone. He sat down and slid a small stack of paper to the bishop: travel documents. Quentin was free to move about within the country—and free to leave Burma! Bishop Quentin Huang resolved that his next step would be America.

May 1950, America: Quentin

Leaving China proved to be the right choice for Quentin. Between October 1949 and the end of 1952, the Communist regime in China killed 186,069 Christians and imprisoned 390,420.

However, when the bishop arrived in California, it was not quite what he expected. Along with Quentin, thousands were fleeing China with many heading to America. These included intellectuals, professionals, and businesspeople. For many, California was their first stop.

The history of Chinese immigrants in California was tumultuous dating back to the mid-nineteenth century during the Gold Rush, and later the building of the Transcontinental Railroad. While the Chinese provided much-needed labor, public sentiment quickly turned against them. Competition for jobs and a depression in the 1870s all led to a racist backlash against the Chinese. Eventually Chinese immigration was ended with the 1882 Chinese Exclusion Act.

The attack on Pearl Harbor on December 7, 1941, changed some, but not all, of these dynamics. California was the epicenter of the U.S.'s anti-Chinese feelings. While China became an ally during the war, many in California clung to their pre-war sentiments. During the war, 13,499 Chinese fought for the United States, 22 percent of all Chinese men in America. Of those that served, 70 percent were in the U.S. Army serving in the 3rd and 4th Infantry Divisions in Europe and the 6th, 32nd, and 77th Infantry Divisions in the Pacific. In the U.S. Army Air Force, 22 percent of the people who served were Chinese. On the home front, the Chinese community contributed money to the Red Cross and ran bond drives to fund the war. In San Francisco, they raised $18,000 for the Red Cross and bought $30,000 in war bonds in 1942 alone.

Despite all of these contributions, Bishop Huang found California to be less than welcoming. While many Californians offered warmth and hospitality, the government and society were buckling under the strain of so many refugees.

The bishop used his connections with church leaders across the country to work with politicians at the highest levels to establish his legal standing within the country. He then began several years of lecturing across America.

1950–55, Gibsonia, Pennsylvania: Janet and Eliza

The 1950s were a magical time for Janet and Eliza at their home in Gibsonia. They continued to produce art which was installed across the country with a special emphasis on ecclesiastical work that was installed in churches, religious schools, and other buildings.

They also cultivated the simple home into a welcoming retreat with gardens and lush landscaping surrounding the three ponds. Many visitors quietly came and went enjoying the surroundings in peace and anonymity.

Anne Morrow Lindberg was a frequent visitor through the years, continuing the warm relationship she had established with them at Cranbook more than a dozen years earlier.

Alexander Calder was a guest as well. Calder was known for his innovative mobiles that brought grace and movement to the world of art. Many people also know him for his monumental public sculptures.

George Nakashima, a sculptor, was another frequent guest. Nakashima was a woodworker, architect, and furniture maker who was one of the leading innovators of twentieth-century furniture design and a father of the American craft movement. He not only came with his intellect and aesthetic sensibility, he brought them wood to use for their sculptures.

Also making the occasional visit was another person who made his mark on the Western Pennsylvania landscape: Frank Lloyd Wright. Wright's iconic home, Falling Water, that he designed for the Kaufman family, is located just an hour southeast of Janet and Eliza's home.

The artistry and accomplishments that passed through the door rivaled any museum in any city.

Alexander Calder (1898–1976) with one of his mobiles. These delicate but vibrant works are often imitated today by other artists.

1954, Washington, D.C.: Quentin

Quentin's life in 1954 was satisfying but not settled. He served as the associate rector at the Church of St. Stephen and the Incarnation in Washington, D.C. The church, founded in 1925, was situated just off 16th St. Northwest, three miles north of the White House.

His timing was historic. For its first thirty years, St. Stephen and the Incarnation was the typical white, middle-class church. Its calendar was marked with choir practice, dances, bridge luncheons, and study groups. The neighborhood changed, and in the 1950s, it became the first integrated Episcopal church in Washington.

The bishop must have felt it to be an amazing juxtaposition practicing his faith so close to the center of government after coming from a land where the government was fixated on removing religion from people's lives.

Later, the church would become active in the civil rights and anti-war movements, as well as many local concerns. When Martin Luther King, Jr., was slain and riots erupted a block away on 14th Street, within hours, St. Stephen's was the site for the first requiem Eucharist for Dr. King. Paul Moore, then the bishop of Washington, wrote: "The church was so full that people coming in could hardly find a place to stand, yet when the prayers began a reverent silence enveloped the congregation, and we could plainly hear the wail of sirens, the sound of gunshots, and the fearsome sound of men running as fast as they could, soles beating on the pavement."

In the early 1970s, St. Stephen's was at the forefront of efforts in the Episcopal Church to allow women to be ordained as priests.

On November 10, 1974, the Rev. Alison Cheek stood before the altar of St. Stephen and the Incarnation Church, said the words, "On the night before he died for us, our Lord Jesus Christ broke bread," and thus launched the public ministry of Episcopal women priests. Up until that moment, no woman had publicly celebrated the Eucharist in an Episcopal Church.

While Quentin spent time in Washington, D.C., he also traveled extensively. Late in 1954, he undertook a trip to lecture and speak, which had him present more than twenty times over a ten-day period across three states explaining the Communist's attack on faith, and in particular Christianity.

His last speech was to 125 people at the Trinity Church in Red Bank, New Jersey. His message was simple: "Communism is in total conflict with Christianity on both practical and ideological levels."

Despite the satisfaction of delivering his message and the warm reception it garnered, Bishop Huang felt the need for a more stable life for himself, Grace Betty and his family. Grace Betty had gone to school to become a nurse to help support the family, and his series of support roles at churches was not sustainable.

He began to reach out to his church network. He was able to reconnect with a man that he had attended seminary school with decades earlier. That man gave him an offer to come to a place that would be both welcoming and stable. The bishop was heading to Pittsburgh.

St. Stephen and the Incarnation Church as it appears today.

1956–1957, Pennsylvania: Janet and Eliza

The latter half of the 1950s was a time of professional success, community involvement, and changing family dynamics for Eliza and Janet.

In 1956, they held a highly regarded joint show at the 130 Gallery in Pittsburgh. Known for its role in the post-war art scene, the gallery was an important space for contemporary and avant-garde art in the region. It provided a platform for both emerging and established artists to showcase their work, contributing to the cultural and artistic development of Pittsburgh during that era. The show consisted of twenty-two pieces and was complemented by photographs showing their work for churches, schools, and other architectural projects.

For Janet, the show included:

> Two statues of saints for St. Scholastic Church in the Aspinwall neighborhood of Pittsburgh. (The sanctuary already held three of her other works.)

A pair of teak wood and bronze doors for Saint Anne's Church in Palo Alto California.
A large panel for the chapel of Saint Margaret's Hospital in Pittsburgh.

For Eliza, it featured:

A stainless-steel Saint Edmunds figure outside of Saint Edmund's school at Church of the Redeemer, in Pittsburgh.
A series of animal panels for a Leechburg school playground in Leechburg, Pennsylvania.
A fountain for the Butler High School in Butler, Pennsylvania.

At the show, Janet showed *Head of Young Christ* in limestone and Eliza showed *Psalm of David.*

Their involvement in the local church also continued. In 1956, the Pine Creek Mission became a parish (meaning they were financially self-sufficient) and the name was changed to St. Thomas Church in the Fields.

As the church grew, the need for a larger building became evident. Eliza, who was already heavily involved in real estate in the area, began exploring options. She noticed a large piece of land east of their home on Dickey Road near State Route 8 (formerly the Butler Plank Road).

She approached the Foy family who also happened to be parishioners at the church. "Would you sell us land?" Eliza asked.

"No," Mr. Foy replied. "But, I'll give you five acres!"

Plans for the new church began in 1957 with architect John Perkuhn leading the design. Perkuhn was born in Steubenville, Ohio, in 1915. He graduated from the Carnegie Institute of Technology and attended Harvard University. After his education, he was the head of architecture for Norman Bell Geddes in New York. He came to Pittsburgh in 1947, opened his own practice, and began teaching at his old school, Carnegie Tech.

It is likely that Janet and Eliza's connections to the school brought him to the project. He worked in a manner that was considered modern and ranged from understated to expressive. His design for the new church was later featured in a number of architectural publications.

Tragically, these happy days were marred by tragedy. Barbara, Eliza's sister, who had married Oscar Sheffler, passed away in 1957 at the age of thirty-nine.

The family still had their father, but Eliza became an even more meaningful part of their life, especially for Peter, the youngest, only seven at the time. The arrangement had the same warmth and love as when Eliza and Janet had served as live-in nannies for Anne Morrow Lindbergh and her children during World War II while teaching at the Cranbrook Academy of Art in Michigan.

Peter Sheffler would later describe his aunt as playful and imaginative, while being "incredibly loving with a great enthusiasm for life." He went on to say: "Her approach was to be there for people. She came at everything through the heart."

Above left: Janet DeCoux by Samuel Stevens Hood, 1956. (*Photo used with permission by the estate of Samuel Stevens Hood*)

Above right: Eliza Miller by Samuel Stevens Hood ,1956. (*Photo used with permission by the estate of Samuel Stevens Hood*)

Eliza creating pieces from her sketch for the stainless steel sculpture of Saint Edmund. (*Photo used with permission by the estate of Samuel Stevens Hood*)

Students holding a pageant in front of the stainless-steel Saint Edmund figure created by Eliza outside of Saint Edmund's school at Church of the Redeemer, in Pittsburgh. (*Photo used with permission by Saint Edmunds School*)

1957–58, Pittsburgh: Quentin

By the late 1950s, hundreds of thousands of people from across Asia had been displaced by war and political unrest. Several thousand of those had settled or were staying temporarily in the Pittsburgh area. Bishop Quentin Huang was one of those people.

Working with the Episcopal Church in the region, Bishop Huang opened the first Oriental Center in Pittsburgh in October 1957. He said: "We want to help these people in any way possible—there is a job to be done teaching democracy. And while it is said Orientals don't understand our life here, there are misconceptions on both sides."

Despite the sponsorship of the Episcopal Church, the center was designed to be non-denominational. "What this center will be is a non-denominational bridge spreading the good and truth of all of the churches—whether it be the love of Christ, the Zen of Confucius, or the mercy of Gautama Buddha," the bishop said.

Quentin found a location for the center in a rented home in Pittsburgh's Shadyside neighborhood. The look of the home was decidedly Victorian with a turret anchoring the right side of the structure, and a heavily bracketed porch marking the left side of the third story. The center included a large meeting room, a ping-pong room, a reading room, and a badminton court. The kitchen was also thoughtfully stocked with cooking utensils specifically for different Asian cuisines, and members of the community were encouraged to come and cook.

During that time, the bishop also found a home for himself and his family. Just a few blocks away, a stunning Tudor home had been built for a successful construction and

The bishop and Grace Betty later in life. (*Photo courtesy of Alice Huang*)

building products magnate named Henry J. Miller (no relation to Eliza). The home was designed by a local noted architect, Frederick J. Osterling. The twin-gabled house was built in the Tudor style with a brick first story and decorative half-timbering above, and a wealth of hardwood within. The house was later owned by Robert Edwin Withers, a treasurer of the Aluminum Co. of America whose father became U.S. consul general in Hong Kong.

The Withers family deeded it to Calvary Episcopal Church with the hope that they could find a fitting resident for the home.

The Oriental Center slowly gained popularity, and the bishop began to spread the word that he was looking for donations so that a permanent center could be built.

1959, Gibsonia, Pennsylvania: Janet & Eliza

Ground was broken for the new Saint Thomas in The Fields church in early 1959. The plans created by Perkuhn came to life, resulting in a stunning, modern church. The cost of the building was ambitious for the time, $125,000 (about $6 million today).

The furnishings were specifically designed and constructed for the new facility, and, of course, Janet and Eliza lent their talents. Eliza designed the pulpit and the lectern. The altar, cross, and candlesticks were designed by Janet. The altar itself was remarkable; it was constructed from a solid piece of granite from Canada's Laurentian Mountains. The wooden cross and figure of Christ were a collaboration of the two: the cross and body of Christ were carved by Janet, and the metal crown was the work of Eliza.

In addition to their work on the church, both kept developing new pieces, and in the winter of 1959, the Carnegie Institute awarded an artist with a show of her own; this time, it was Eliza.

The show consisted of both new and older pieces. The ones created in past years included works made from terracotta, carved slate, bronze, enamel, and steel. Her newer works featured hammered metal and welded metal. The newer works were considered some of her finest.

The *Pittsburgh Post-Gazette* reported: "Here is an artist who combines a poetic imagination with a pragmatic discipline which insists that each type of sculptural material yield up its special kind of image, sometimes witty and informal but oftener spiritual in its implications."

Some of the pieces garnering the most attention were *Adam and Eve* and *Cain and Abel*, which were hammered from steel plates using the same technique as medieval armor makers. Crowds also formed around *Cat*, *Head*, *Andel that Troubled the Waters*, and *The Golden Shepherd*.

During this time, Eliza began to use her portion of the family fortune to expand her interests in real estate. While the old Butler Plank Road had long been converted to a more modern highway, the Butler Shortline Railroad, which served as the trolley line to Pittsburgh, had been removed and not replaced. The area remained more agricultural than residential, and Eliza took the opportunity to begin purchasing large tracts of land and individual lots. She sold some, held some, and even provided land (either free or at greatly discounted prices) to other writers and artists. She even used her wealth to assist in home building for some, and often lent her artistic, engineering, and design skills to construction projects. She quietly became one of the largest landowners in the area.

Above: Expansive glass is a signature of Saint Thomas in the Fields.

Below: The bell tower was designed by Janet.

The crucifix designed by Janet.

1959–1961, Gibsonia, Pennsylvania: Janet, Eliza, and Quentin

In late 1959, Bishop Thomas invited Bishop Quentin Huang to attend an event at one of the churches outside of Pittsburgh. The car ride was leisurely and enjoyable, and while the landscape was not nearly as mountainous as that of Kunming, Quentin may have found some comfort and familiarity in the verdant hills and towering trees as they headed north.

When they arrived at the church, Quentin was struck by the stunning architecture. It was not overly embellished and ornate like other cathedrals; its simple clean angles and open spaces allowed for reflection and simplicity. The church was Saint Thomas in the Fields in Gibsonia.

After the service, a small gathering was held, and a member of the church suggested that there were two people who might greatly enjoy the bishop's company and his story. Quentin was introduced to Janet DeCoux and Eliza Miller.

Over the course of several hours, Quentin thoughtfully told his story to Eliza and Janet. They were spellbound, and the trio immediately bonded over their shared beliefs. They talked of travel and adventure. They talked of family. They talked of challenges and accomplishments. They talked of loss. They talked of faith.

Quentin also relayed his current predicament; he could see all sides of the issues that he faced at the Oriental Center and was seeking a way forward. For the Asian community, they needed an environment to learn about democracy, the value of freedom, and the uniquely American opportunity to be untethered in the practice of faith. For the American community, Chinese culture was being unfairly equated to the new Communist regimes that were emerging on the other side of the world. How could he show the beauty of Asian culture, its intellect, and introspective nature? He knew that very few people from this part of the country would ever experience China in any way other than seeing a picture in a book, and while the greater Pittsburgh community had accepted him and his family, how could he truly express how his upbringing and environment had shaped him?

No record exists of when they idea came to Eliza and Janet, but events show that they moved quickly to help the bishop resolve these issues.

Eliza gifted him nearly 7 acres tucked away in a wooded area and helped the bishop financially and logistically to create a new place that would not only serve as his home, but also as the new Oriental Center. Janet and Eliza provided their thoughts on the layout and arrangement of the structures and were an endless source of construction knowledge and connections.

In a little more than a year, the home and gardens took shape at the end of a long driveway extending from a dead-end street.

The red brick home featured a clay-tiled roof with the corners gracefully tilting toward the sky. Octagonal windows flanked the front door, and the walls were made up of brick and stone. The house was separated by the garage with a 7-foot-tall moon gate. The ground featured elaborate gardens, a three-level tower called a pagoda, and a small fishpond. A stunning arch adorned with Chinese characters marked the beginning of the property at the driveway.

This was the home that I would discover, and rediscover, years later.

The front of the home shortly after completion. (*Photo courtesy of Peter Sheffler*)

The moon gate from the front. (*Photo courtesy of Peter Sheffler*)

The rear of the moon gate. (*Photo courtesy of Peter Sheffler*)

A structure called a "ting ze" provides a place for contemplation. (*Photo courtesy of Peter Sheffler*)

Ornamentation on the ting ze. (*Photo courtesy of Peter Sheffler*)

The ting ze with the house in the distance. (*Photo courtesy of Peter Sheffler*)

Left: The pagoda. (*Photo courtesy of Peter Sheffler*)

Below: The arch at the end of the driveway. (*Photo courtesy of Peter Sheffler*)

Above left: The left side of the arch. (*Photo courtesy of Peter Sheffler*)

Above right: The right side of the arch. (*Photo courtesy of Peter Sheffler*)

The circular moon gate can be seen between the house and garage. (*Photo courtesy of Peter Sheffler*)

1962–1968, Gibsonia: Janet, Eliza, and Quentin

The 1960s were a wonderful time of family, community, and, of course, art for Janet, Eliza, and Quentin.

Janet and Eliza's home grew to showcase their taste in art as well as their diverse interests. Scattered through the house was an eclectic mix of inspirational items including a collection of pottery and ancient terra cotta from Persia, China, and pre-Columbian America.

The sunroom featured a modern shelf system designed and built by Janet to hold the items they collected from around their world. When asked about her acquisition strategy, Janet smiled and remarked: "If we like the design we don't care what period a thing is."

The living room featured a carved wooden figure, a female form that they had discovered in an antique shop in Maryland. "We believe a missionary brought it here," Eliza said. It had a grass skirt, and Janet and Eliza would keep it in place or remove it to highlight the work depending on the nature of their visitors.

Other remarkable items around the home included: a horse from the T'ang Dynasty; an Ethiopian incensor; bowls and vases from Cambodia and Peru; an old, exquisite French clock; small Eskimo dolls; a percussion instrument from Addis Ababa used in Coptic religious celebrations; American Indian rugs; a lithograph by Mexican artist Tomaya; and a large collection of books.

The furnishings were a mix of old and new. Many were collected by her parents. Janet said of her father: "He just went around to secondhand shops and auctions and bought furniture to fill the rooms. He just had a feeling for antiques"

Since Janet and Eliza both knew wood and metal so well, when they needed other furniture, they simply made what they wanted.

Both were avid gardeners, too. The grounds featured three large spring-fed ponds, and they crafted a park-like retreat around them with lilac bushes and dogwood trees. To these, Janet and Eliza added hundreds of pine trees and shrubs. The grounds also featured a number of their sculptures, most notably *Sarah and Abraham* created by Janet and a whimsical fish sculpture by Eliza.

The barn was divided into two studio spaces, and it was not unusual to see one of them working with a bandsaw or welder. The structure sat back from the road, and Eliza thought its placement suited them well. "Sometimes we make a lot of noise."

Eliza continued to expand her real estate holdings in the area, and her portfolio even included a mansion. In 1928, her parents purchased a sprawling house in Talbot County, Maryland, known as Emerson Point from the Seth Family. Ownership transferred to Eliza in 1964, and she would maintain control for decades to come.

Their house on Dickey Road and studio became a stop on garden tours and school field trips, and not surprisingly, the bishop and Mrs. Huang's home was a stop as well. What a contrast; one of the area's oldest homes and a compound from China that seemed to come from the pages of *National Geographic*! Eliza's nephew, Peter Sheffler, remembers visiting the bishop's home during that time period. They celebrated Chinese New Year, ate Chinese vegetables, and enjoyed a dish known as bird's nest soup. Guests even stretched their culinary pallets further with a Chinese dish called "hundred-year-old egg."

The tours also often included a stop across the street at the home of Janet's sister and her husband, Paul Simpson. Paul also studied at Carnegie Tech; his field was architecture rather than art, and he also studied architecture in Europe under a Le Brun Scholarship. He designed the Food Building for the World's Fair and was an assistant to Raymond Hood during the design of Rockefeller Center. Their home featured stunning architecture and even a mobile designed by Calder.

It was Paul who ultimately brought one of Janet's largest opportunities to her.

While her accolades were for her religious works, she had shown great abilities in a variety of media, including limestone, granite, slate, marble, wood, and bronze. Her representational pieces had an uncluttered aesthetic, blending Modernism with an appreciation of the human figure.

The executive director of the Pennsylvania Historical Commission, S. K. Steven, proposed a project that would house both a museum and the archive of William Penn, the founder of Pennsylvania. He thought the project should include a statue of William Penn. For that he needed a sculptor. When he heard that no artist had been selected, Paul Simpson then serving as an architect for Lawrie and Green suggested Janet.

Steven agreed, and in 1962, Janet began the work. Admittedly, she knew nothing about William Penn. "Like many other Pennsylvanians, I had heard about him so much I had always just assumed I knew about him till I was faced with the situation." Her foremost concern was "how to relate the statue to something I truly believe in, and still not compromise it."

Steven offered her a copy of the book *Remember William Penn*. She felt an immediate connection upon reading the opening paragraphs: "At eighteen William Penn, founder of Pennsylvania, was expelled from Oxford because he was too religious ... [he] put ahead of all things the conscience of the individual, in whom he saw shining the Inner Light of God."

First, she completed a 9-inch study which showed Penn with his head tilted slightly downward and feet apart creating a sense of movement. A small figure in Quaker costume was superimposed on his chest, hands raised in a gesture of praise. Penn holds his hand over the figure, symbolizing his protection of "Free Man" and freedom of religion. Over the next few years, the figure was enlarged to 18 inches, then to 3 feet, and then to 6 feet.

After acquiring the final approval, the figure was then enlarged to a 17-foot, 6-inch model in 1964 made from plaster. Eliza's nephew, Peter Sheffler, vividly recalls the statue taking shape in the barn behind their home.

The plaster version was sent to Mexico City to the foundry Fundicion Artistica. The piece was finally installed in the museum in 1965.

Today, the William Penn statue remains a focal point of the State Museum of Pennsylvania. It is a site of frequent visitors and tours. Schoolchildren on field trips rub the statue's shoes as they walk by, so much so that the patina on Penn's feet has been burnished away.

Janet rather liked that experience, saying, "I've thought a lot about the children who will visit that great museum building and see the statue in future years.... I hope it will have meaning for them—the same kind of meaning that William Penn has for me. That's why I've worked to give it a sense of mystery. Kids are interested in the unknown. Maybe it's because they haven't learned to be in too much of a hurry to consider the important things."

Above left: Janet in her studio working on William Penn.

Above right: The State Museum of Pennsylvania.

Just a year later, Janet created one of her smaller works. A young man by the name of Neil Riley grew up in Gibsonia. He played football, wrestled, and ran track. He loved his dog and spent countless days hunting and fishing in the woods—and he wanted to be a U.S. Marine.

He joined the Marines and was killed less than a month after arriving in Vietnam in February 1966. After his death at Phu Bai, his classmates at the local high school asked Janet to create a plaque for him. The bronze plaque was dedicated May 30, 1967, and rededicated when a new high school was built nearly thirty years later.

Janet and Eliza did other projects as well. Eliza created a series of enamel on steel panels for Duquesne University. Janet created a statue of St. Stephen for a church in Sewickley Pennsylvania of the same name, and Eliza created a large, three-part sundial sculpture for the Ellis School in Shadyside, Pennsylvania.

In the later 1960s, the leadership of Saint Thomas of the Fields began plans to add a chapel to the church as a sacred place for parishioners to have a Christian burial.

Janet's sister, Marion, and her husband, Paul Simpson, designed and created the stained-glass windows. (It was their first time creating stained glass!) The top of the altar table was crafted by a man named Bob Salvatora based upon a design by Janet. The top itself was made from an oak tree recovered from a peat bog in Ireland. It was thought to be over 2,000 old and was alive at the time of Christ.

Eliza and Janet also created vestments for St. Thomas along with another relative, Barbara Luderowski. (Barbara would later go on to establish a renowned art gallery in Pittsburgh known as The Mattress Factory.)

The walnut cross from the original Pine Creek church was hung on the wall of the chapel, and by 1968, the Chapel of the Resurrection was completed.

Sadly, it would become a greater part of this story just a few years later.

July 2, 1973, Gibsonia, Pennsylvania

The first days of July 1973 brought that familiar anticipation of the celebration of freedom, and nobody appreciated that freedom more than Quentin. But he never saw the fireworks that year. On July 2, 1973, Bishop Quentin Huang passed away at the age of seventy-one.

A service was held in Trinity Cathedral in downtown Pittsburgh. It was presided over by his friend, Reverend William Thomas.

He was interred in the Chapel of the Resurrection at St. Thomas in the Fields Church.

1974, Gibsonia, Pennsylvania: The Author

Peter Sheffler's girlfriend served as an interim caretaker for the property after the death of Quentin. One day she saw a group of small boys wandering around the property. She decided to offer them a friendly greeting and show them around the grounds. One of the boys, the youngest of the group, happened to be particularly fascinated by the home and gardens.

That young boy was me.

1987, Gibsonia, Pennsylvania: The Author

As the 1980s slowly enveloped the country, the days of my childhood were blotted away by the events, culture, and the inevitability of leaving for college. I was fortunate to go. Many kids in those years did not. My father saved relentlessly, and my mother even put aside the comfort and success she enjoyed as a homemaker, part-time cake decorator, and part-time landscape painter to re-enter the working world full-time to help pay for college.

Those years were truly unique: John Lennon was gunned down on the steps of his apartment. Mount St. Helens erupted, covering much of the country in ash. Ronald Reagan became president. Michael Jackson released "Thriller." Robert Ballard probed the depths of the Atlantic to finally find the *Titanic*. Chernobyl suffered an apocalyptic meltdown. The Space Shuttle *Challenger* exploded shortly after takeoff and made America weep. The Berlin Wall came down and the world rejoiced.

Under the canopy of those events, I continued to fish on occasion. I was not especially good at it, but I enjoyed the quiet, and each fish was carefully returned to the water.

As the decade passed, my wanderings expanded as I looked for new ponds. One afternoon, I traversed several large expanses of woods and came to a series of connected ponds nestled among an old farmhouse, a large barn and several outbuildings. It took me more than fifty years to make the connection that I was fishing on Janet and Eliza's property.

While I was outside fishing, they were inside working.

I had the chance to meet them but never knew it.

Pittsburgh today. Carnegie Mellon lies behind and to the right of the tall buildings.

Right: Janet and Eliza's house today tucked in a thick stand of trees. (*Photo: Weiss, 2024*)

Below: Janet and Eliza's studio today. (*Photo: Weiss, 2024*)

2
Final Notes

A story like this covering so many historical figures leaves many loose ends. Properly concluding each and truly illuminating their historic and cultural significance would require a second book. Here are just a few notes to provide closure where possible:

Janet DeCoux (1904–1999)

Janet passed away in 1999 at the age of ninety-five. Her writings, sketches, and other materials including her correspondence with Anne Morrow Lindberg are held in the Smithsonian.

Eliza Miller (1914–2007)

Eliza passed away in 2007 at the age of ninety-two after a long illness. In addition to her substantial contribution to the arts, she was an avid real estate investor, and at one time was the second largest landowner in the Gibsonia area. She was exceedingly generous and was known to help writers and artists with the acquisition of land and the building of homes.

Alice Huang (1937–Present)

The number of amazing people connected with this story is almost endless. Alice Huang, the bishop's daughter, and her husband, David Baltimore, are two of those people.

Alice was born in China during the Japanese invasion, and the Nanking Massacre, also known as the Rape of Nanking, in 1937. (Note, you will see both "Nanjing" and "Nanking" in various works. Nanjing being the modern spelling and Nanking being the traditional spelling.) Nanking is only 300 miles northeast of her birth city, Nanchang, in Jiangxi province.

She spent much of her youth and teenage years voyaging around the world with her parents, but by 1957, she was at Wellesley College in Massachusetts, and two years later was at medical school at Johns Hopkins in Baltimore. She was fascinated by research and began studying viruses with the hope of understanding how cells fight viruses.

While presenting a conference paper, she met David Baltimore, an emerging researcher.

David was born in 1938 in New York City and attended Great Neck High School, where he developed an interest in biology, particularly animal behavior. He studied molecular biology at Swarthmore College where he graduated with a degree in chemistry in 1960. He then attended the Massachusetts Institute of Technology (MIT), where he worked as a research assistant under the guidance of Herman Kalckar, a noted biochemist.

During one instance where their paths crossed, Alice asked David's opinion on joining Jonas Salk to do research. David's advice to Alice was simple: "Don't work with Jonas Salk. Work with me!" What an offer! Shortly after that, Alice began working with David researching viral replication. After relocating with David to MIT, Alice and David were married in October 1968.

The team of Huang and Baltimore along with a graduate student named Stampfer made important discoveries in the process of replication. However, Alice studied the history of other women researchers and decided that it was important to have recognition for her own research and began working at Harvard Medical School.

In 1975, David Baltimore was awarded the Nobel Prize jointly with Howard Temin and Renato Dulbecco for discoveries concerning the interaction between tumor viruses and the genetic material of the cell. Yes, a Nobel Prize.

Although she enjoyed her time at Harvard, Alice was offered the position as the dean of science at New York University. The synchronicity was remarkable; David was named the president of Rockefeller University at the same time. Alice accepted the challenge and served as the dean for science for six years (1991–1997).

After their time in New York, the couple headed to the West Coast when David became the president of the California Institute of Technology at Pasadena, California, in 1997 (also referred to as CalTech and CIT). Alice became the senior councilor for external relations, as well as a faculty associate in biology at CIT. Alice was also known as "the First Lady of CIT."

The record of Alice's achievement is truly amazing. She has been receiving awards since her time at Wellesley College—twenty-seven awards and honors from 1958 to 2001. She has been a member of twelve professional societies, has chaired forty-two meetings of various kinds, served on editorial boards, and has an admirable record in community service.

She has authored 120 professional publications, and she has been an invaluable resource for the creation of this book.

Above and below: Alice's snapshots of her parent's home. (*Photo courtesy of Alice Huang*)

Visitors to Janet and Eliza's Home

Anne Morrow Lindbergh (1906–2001)

An acclaimed American author and aviator, she was known for her literary works and pioneering flights with her husband, Charles Lindbergh. She authored *Gift from the Sea*, reflecting on life and womanhood. Her contributions to aviation and literature made her a notable figure in American history.

Frank Lloyd Wright (1867–1959)

A pioneering American architect, he was known for his innovative designs and use of materials. His notable works include Fallingwater and the Guggenheim Museum. Wright's integration of buildings with their natural surroundings and his revolutionary use of space profoundly influenced modern architecture.

George Nakashima (1905–1990)

A renowned American woodworker and furniture maker, Nakashima was celebrated for his craftsmanship and use of natural wood. His designs emphasized organic beauty and simplicity, blending traditional Japanese techniques with modern aesthetics.

Annie Dillard (1945–)

A cousin of Peter Sheffler, Annie is a Pulitzer Prize-winning American author known for her narrative prose and keen observations of nature and spirituality. Her acclaimed works, including *Pilgrim at Tinker Creek*, explore themes of existence and the natural world, making her a significant figure in contemporary literature.

Alexander Calder (1898–1976)

Alexander Calder was born on July 22, 1898, in Lawnton, Pennsylvania, near Harrisburg. Perhaps being an artist was destiny. His father, Alexander Stirling Calder, was a noted sculptor, and his mother, Nanette Lederer Calder, was a professional portrait artist. Calder's grandfather, Alexander Milne Calder, was also a well-known sculptor whose works included the monumental statue of William Penn that crowns Philadelphia's City Hall. (The second giant William Penn connected to this story!)

Despite his family's artistic background, Calder initially pursued a different path, attending the Stevens Institute of Technology in Hoboken, New Jersey, where he studied mechanical engineering. He graduated in 1919 and then worked as a draftsman and hydraulic engineer.

His passion for art ultimately drew him back to the creative world.

In 1923, Calder enrolled at the Art Students League in New York City, where he studied painting and drawing. During this time, he also worked as an illustrator, notably for the *National Police Gazette*, where he developed his eye for whimsical and energetic compositions. Calder's fascination with movement and mechanics began to surface in these early years, though it would be several more years before he fully embraced sculpture as his primary medium.

In 1926, Calder moved to Paris, where he became involved with the avant-garde art community. It was here that he made one of his first significant breakthroughs, creating a miniature circus, *Cirque Calder*. Using wire, cloth, wood, and other simple materials, Calder crafted a series of miniature figures and animals that he could manipulate to perform for audiences. His *Cirque Calder* was a kinetic, performative work that foreshadowed many of the themes—motion, playfulness, and interaction—that would define his later work.

This Parisian period also marked Calder's introduction to abstract art. He was influenced by the work of Piet Mondrian, whose use of geometric forms and primary colors made a profound impact on him. Although Calder briefly considered becoming a painter in Mondrian's abstract style, he soon realized that his true calling lay in three-dimensional form.

In 1931, Calder made the pivotal decision to abandon traditional sculpture and embrace movement as a key element of his art. He created a series of motorized works that moved mechanically. These early kinetic sculptures, which were dubbed "mobiles" by artist Marcel Duchamp, marked the birth of a new genre. Unlike the static sculptures of his predecessors, Calder's mobiles were designed to move, creating ever-changing compositions through the interplay of form, balance, and motion.

How important was the year 1931 to Calder? That same year, he married Louisa James, with whom he would have two daughters.

Calder's mobiles were a radical departure from traditional sculpture. Made from wire, metal, and wood, these sculptures were suspended in the air, where they could rotate and sway in response to air currents. The delicate balance of the elements, combined with their ability to move unpredictably, gave Calder's work a sense of life and dynamism that had never been seen in sculpture before. His mobiles were not only aesthetically pleasing but also interactive, as they engaged with their surroundings and changed depending on environmental conditions.

Calder's mobiles varied in scale, from small tabletop pieces to large public installations. His ability to manipulate form and balance allowed him to create works that seemed to defy gravity, with elements floating and rotating in space with surprising grace and fluidity. Many of his mobiles were abstract in form, drawing inspiration from nature—he often likened them to trees, clouds, or the movement of planets.

In addition to his mobiles, Calder also developed a related form of sculpture, the "stabile." While his mobiles were defined by their movement, the stabiles were static sculptures, often monumental in size. These large, abstract forms were constructed from sheet metal and painted in bold colors. Though they did not move like the mobiles, the stabiles retained a sense of energy and tension, as if they were on the verge of motion.

Throughout the 1940s and 1950s, Calder continued to refine his work, becoming one of the most celebrated sculptors in the world. He exhibited widely in Europe and the United States, and his work was collected by major museums and patrons. During this time, Calder also began creating large-scale public sculptures, many of which were commissioned for outdoor spaces and corporate buildings. These monumental works, often brightly colored and abstract, became iconic features in cities around the world.

One of Calder's most famous public works is *La Grande Vitesse* (1969), a massive red stabile installed in downtown Grand Rapids, Michigan. The sculpture's dynamic, soaring forms have become a symbol of the city, and its installation marked one of the first instances of public art being funded by the U.S. government's Art in Public Places program. Calder's public sculptures, whether mobiles or stabiles, have since become landmarks in cities such as Chicago, Paris, and Washington, D.C.

Calder's influence on modern art cannot be overstated. His introduction of movement into sculpture revolutionized the medium, paving the way for later developments in kinetic and interactive art. Artists such as Jean Tinguely and George Rickey were directly influenced by Calder's pioneering work with moving sculptures, and his approach to form and color had a profound impact on the development of abstract and minimalist art in the twentieth century.

In addition to his sculptural work, Calder was also a prolific printmaker and designed stage sets, jewelry, and tapestries. His work across various media reflected his boundless creativity and curiosity, as well as his desire to explore the relationships between form, movement, and space.

In 1976, Calder's work was the subject of a major retrospective at the Whitney Museum of American Art in New York City.

He passed away just two weeks after the opening on November 11, 1976.

Other Figures in the Book:

Shirley Carter Hughson (1867–1949)

An American religious leader and scholar, he was notably a member of the Order of the Holy Cross, an Anglican monastic community. He contributed significantly to the revival of monastic life in the Episcopal Church and authored several works on spirituality and religious practice. Janet and Father Hugson developed a deep bond, and he was an influential force in her spiritual life up to his death in 1949.

John Perkun (1915–1998)

Accomplished both professionally and academically, Perkun taught at Carnegie Mellon for thirty-two years before retiring in 1979. He was known for primarily his residential designs, but he also designed several religious institutions, including St. Sava's Serb. Orthodox and St. Edmund's Academy, Pittsburgh.

Samuel Stevens Hood (1917–1959)

The dramatic photographic portraits of Janet and Eliza are the work of photographer Samuel Steven Hood. In addition to his photographic work, he was a reporter and a musician. He worked at *The Press*, a Scripps-Howard daily paper in Pittsburgh, and had previously worked at a Harrisburg paper.

Hood was a gifted pianist and was *The Press*'s art critic—one of the most controversial figures in Pittsburgh art circles. He was on his way back to the newspaper offices when he was killed by a runaway bus that crashed into a crowd of people on a downtown corner in 1959. After his death, his photos were given to the Carnegie Museum of Art by his wife, Elizabeth Wallace Hood. She passed away in 1995.

Janet's Mentors (1927–1930)

Aristide Berto Cianfarani (1895–1960)

Cianfarani was born in 1895 and came to Providence, Rhode Island, in 1913. He studied for three years at the Rhode Island School of Design, under another Italian-born sculptor, Antonio Cirino. After his education, he served in the U.S. Army Signal Corps during World War I. When he returned from the war, he began working as a sculptor and eventually opened his own studio in 1926. Cianfarani was most noted for his large works. Throughout his career, he created monuments and war memorials. He also created a bust of Abraham Lincoln nearly 6 feet tall for an Italian competition and later assisted in the creation of the Borg Warner Trophy for the winner of the Indianapolis 500. It was first awarded in 1936 by the owner of the speedway, World War I flying ace Eddie Rickenbacker.

Alvin Mayer (1892–1968)

Trained at the American Academy in Rome, the Maryland Institute of Art, and the Pennsylvania Academy of the Fine Arts, Meyer was a student of Paul Manship and a winner of the Prix de Rome. He executed sculptures on a number of Chicago landmarks, including the Board of Trade Building in the downtown Loop area, and the *Chicago Daily News* building on Riverside Plaza, one of Chicago's great public places.

Gozo Kawamura (1884–1959)

Kawamura was born in Nagano, Japan, in 1884. He came to America and settled in New York in 1906. He studied at the National Academy of Design and graduated in 1909. He invented an enlarging machine that helped construct significant monumental sculptures in the U.S., including the statue *The Contemplation of Justice* at the U.S. Supreme Court and several major public works in New York City. He went to create busts of President Calvin Coolidge, General Douglas MacCarthur, and others.

James Earle Fraser (1876–1953)

Fraser's ancestors on his mother's side can be traced back to the Plymouth Pilgrims. His father, Thomas Fraser, was an engineer who worked for railroad companies as they expanded across the American West. A few months before his son was born, Thomas Fraser was one of a group of men sent to recover the remains of the 7th Cavalry Regiment following George Armstrong Custer's disastrous engagement with the Lakota, Cheyenne, and Arapaho forces at the Battle of the Little Bighorn. As a child, Fraser began carving figures from pieces of limestone scavenged from a stone quarry close to his home near Mitchell, South Dakota, in early life. He attended classes at the School of the Art Institute of Chicago in 1890 and studied at the École des Beaux Arts and the Académie Julian in Paris in the late nineteenth century.

Whitney Warren (1864–1943)

Whitney Warren was born in 1864 in New York City, and perhaps had a bit of a head start in life. His grandfather, Stephen Whitney, amassed a considerable fortune in the early 1800s through various shipping and export businesses. In 1830, Stephen was named as one of New York's five millionaires along with John Jacob Astor, John G. Coster, Nathaniel Prime, and Robert Lenox. He died in 1860 worth just short of $4.5 million (nearly $100 million today).

Whitney studied architecture privately and briefly attended Columbia University before continuing his studies at the École des Beaux-Arts in Paris from 1885 to 1894. The École followed a rigorous curriculum that emphasized the classical traditions of architecture, blending formal academic training with hands-on design experience. The Beaux-Arts methodology focused on symmetry, elaborate ornamentation, and grand scale, all of which would become hallmarks of Warren's work.

During his time at the École, Warren developed a deep appreciation for French architectural traditions, particularly the integration of art and design in public spaces. His time in Europe, which also included travels throughout France and Italy, exposed him to Classical and Renaissance architecture, further informing his aesthetic sensibilities. These influences would play a critical role in shaping the direction of his later projects.

When he returned to New York, he worked in the offices of McKim, Mead & White, when he was commissioned to design a country house for the lawyer and amateur architect Charles Delevan Wetmore.

Wetmore was impressed and convinced him to help launch a new venture. In 1898, they established Warren & Wetmore which became one of the most renowned architectural firms of the Gilded Age.

Whitney was the principal designer of the firm and used his social connections to find clients while Wetmore was the legal and financial brain behind the business.

Their projects often catered to the elite, including luxury hotels, apartment buildings, and public monuments. Whitney's European influences were apparent in the firm's work, and the Beaux-Arts style characterized by its monumental facades, intricate detailing, and grand spaces also defined their projects.

One of the firm's most iconic achievements was the design of Grand Central Terminal in New York City, a project that solidified Warren & Wetmore's status as one of the leading architectural firms of the time. Completed in 1913, Grand Central is a masterpiece of Beaux-Arts architecture, celebrated for its grandeur, symmetry, and the elegance of its interior spaces. The terminal became a symbol of New York City's rise as a global metropolis, and Whitney's contributions to its design are considered one of the crowning achievements of his career.

In addition to his work on high-profile public and private buildings, Whitney was also involved in urban planning. He believed that cities should be designed with the same principles of beauty and order that guided his architectural projects. His work in this area included contributions to the planning of New York City's public spaces, as well as involvement in international projects, such as the rebuilding of Reims Cathedral in France after World War I.

Whitney and his brother, Lloyd, established the Society of Beaux-Arts Architects and the Beaux-Arts Institute of Design, both in New York. The two made quite the pair. Whitney was always dressed for society occasions while Lloyd embraced an eccentric style that included a wardrobe influenced by exotic foreign styles. (Sadly, Lloyd died in 1922 sleepwalking out of a window in Paris.)

Warren's commitment to the principles of the Beaux-Arts movement was unwavering, even as architectural trends began to shift in the years following World War I. He believed that the Classical traditions of architecture provided a foundation for artistic excellence and that the Beaux-Arts style would endure as a symbol of cultural achievement.

He married Charlotte Mead Tooker, and they were the parents of three children.

Whitney Warren died on January 24, 1943.

Appendix I
The Work of Janet, Eliza, and Quentin

While researching this book, I could not find a complete, consolidated list of the artwork for either Janet or Eliza. The list below details some items not referenced in the text. It is not complete; I am certain it is missing many, many things. It should, however, provide an overview of their work. In talking with people at several facilities, I found that a number of their pieces have been moved or placed in storage. If you attempt to go and see their work, you may want to ensure that it is still present before making the trip.

Also, of note, Bishop Quentin Huang was the author of two books. Without these, this book would not have been possible.

Works by Janet

- World War I monument, Providence County Courthouse (1926). Served as an assistant to architect Paul P. Cret and sculptor C. P. Jennewein.
- *Meditation* (1943). A bronze sculpture depicting a contemplative figure in a seated pose.
- Saint Scholastica Church (*circa* 1949). The walnut crucifix and the statues of Mary and St. Joseph in the sanctuary.
- *Mother and Child* (1950). A bronze sculpture capturing the bond between a mother and her child.
- *St. Benedict* (1956). German critic Anton Henze selected the work as one of the United States' notable, recent contributions to Roman Catholic art in his work *Contemporary Church Art*.
- *St. Benedict Holding Raven* (1956). Intended to portray self-sacrifice.
- *Winged Victory* (1957). A sculpture depicting a triumphant figure with outstretched wings.
- *The Dancer* (1965). A bronze sculpture capturing the grace and movement of a dancer in motion.
- *Harvest* (1972). A painting depicting a bountiful harvest scene with agricultural motifs.

- *Family Group* (1980). A bronze sculpture depicting a group of figures representing family dynamics.
- *Seated Nude* (1990). A sculpture portraying a seated female figure in a relaxed pose.
- *Still Life with Flowers* (date unknown). A painting depicting a vibrant arrangement of flowers in a still-life composition.
- *Portrait of a Young Woman* (date unknown). A painting capturing the likeness of a young woman in a portrait format.
- *Serenity* (date unknown). A sculpture depicting a serene figure in a meditative pose.
- *Eve* (date unknown). A metaphorical statue of Eve contemplating the apple.

Janet's work was also on display, or held in the collections of the following institutions:

- Brookgreen Gardens, Murrells Inlet, South Carolina.
- National Academy of Design, New York, New York.
- Smithsonian American Art Museum, Washington, D.C.
- National Gallery of Art, Washington, D.C.
- University of Notre Dame, Snite Museum of Art, Notre Dame, Indiana.
- Harvard University, Harvard Art Museum, Fogg Museum, Cambridge, Massachusetts.
- State Museum of Pennsylvania, Memorial Hall, Harrisburg, Pennsylvania.
- St. Stephen's Episcopal Church, Sewickley, Pennsylvania.
- Sacred Heart Elementary School, Pittsburgh, Pennsylvania.
- Society of Medalists.
- St. Scholastica's Church, Aspinwall, Pennsylvania.
- Rhode Island School of Design, Providence, Rhode Island.
- Birger Sandzen Memorial Gallery, Lindsborg, Kanasa.
- The Metropolitan Museum of Art, New York, New York.

Works by Eliza

A listing of Eliza's work was not available, but her work was on display or held in the collections of the following institutions:

- St. Edmunds School, Pennsylvania.
- St. Scholastica Church, Pennsylvania.
- Leechburg Elementary School, Pennsylvania.
- Woodsdale Temple, Wheeling, West Virginia.
- The Metropolitan Museum of Art, New York, New York.
- The Philadelphia Academy, Philadelphia, Pennsylvania.
- The Syracuse Museum, Syracuse, New York.
- The Detroit Art Institute, Detroit, Michigan.

Awards Won by Eliza

- Associated Artists Annuals.
- The Carnegie Institute Prize.
- Society of Sculptors.
- Arensberg Award.

Books by Bishop Quentin Huang

- *Now I Can Tell*, Morehouse-Gorham Co., New York, 1954.
- *Pilgrim from a Red Land*, published posthumously by Exposition Press, 1981.

Appendix II

More Incredibly Fascinating People Connected to this Story

Jennie Eliza Breneman Kennedy, Eliza Miller's Grandmother (1852–1930)

(Note: Julian Kennedy, Eliza's grandfather, is covered earlier in this book.)

Jennie Kennedy was born as Jane Eliza Breneman in Mahoning County, Ohio, in 1852 to Joseph and Elizabeth Breneman.

She married Julian Kennedy in 1878 and quickly became notable for her efforts to secure women the right to vote. She was one of the founding members of the Equal Franchise Federation of Pittsburgh. Kennedy, Jennie Bradley Roessing, and Mary E. Bakewell created the "Pittsburgh Plan" for women's suffrage strategies in Pennsylvania.

In 1914, she was the leader, known as "the Boss of the Road," for the suffrage parade in Pittsburgh. The event was massive and ended with a rally that included thirty speakers on women's suffrage.

The efforts of her organization were instrumental in building public support that contributed to the eventual passage of the 19th Amendment to the U.S. Constitution in 1920, which granted women the right to vote nationwide.

Her daughters, Lucy Kennedy Miller (Eiza's mother) and Eliza Kennedy Smith (Eliza's aunt), were also active members of the women's suffrage movement. By 1915, Lucy Miller had become president of the Equal Franchise Federation of Pittsburgh while Eliza had been appointed chair of the federation's membership committee.

Jennie E. Kennedy died in St. Petersburg, Florida, during a vacation on February 7, 1930.

Lucy Kennedy Miller, Eliza's Mother (1880–1962)

Lucy Kennedy Miller was born to Julian and Jennie Kennedy in 1880 in Braddock, Pennsylvania. The family would have six children, including Joseph Walker Kennedy (1884–1950), Julian Kennedy (1886–1955), Hugh Truesdale Kennedy (1888–1989), Eliza Jane Kennedy (1889–1964), and Thomas Walker Kennedy (1894–1922).

Sometime around 1892, her parents moved the Kennedy family from Latrobe, Pennsylvania—where her sister, Eliza, was born—to Pittsburgh.

Lucy attended the Winchester Thurston School in Pittsburgh and subsequently graduated from Vassar College in 1902.

She was close to her parents and continued to live with them until 1907 when she married John Oliver Miller. Lucy and John would have three children: Julian Kennedy Miller (1910–2001), Eliza Jane Miller (1914–2007), and Barbara Miller Sheffler (1920–1957).

Several years into her marriage, Lucy joined Pittsburgh's suffrage movement. Her participation grew from simply being an attendee to an influential force in the creation of the Allegheny County Equal Rights Association (later renamed as the Equal Franchise Federation of Western Pennsylvania), becoming the organization's treasurer and then president in 1912. Her position made her a key contact for journalists of the era who were reporting on the suffrage movement.

Her interest in the suffrage movement was well constructed and complex. When interviewed in 1913, she said: "We have been trying to get a children's labor law in Pennsylvania the past 14 years, and the only way we will get it is to get the vote."

Along with Mary Bakewell, she co-founded a school for suffragists. She even recruited teachers from the University of Pittsburgh faculty. In 1914, she orchestrated a parade to celebrate Suffrage Day, and in 1915, on behalf of the Woman Suffrage Party, she wrote an appeal to Pennsylvania voters, urging them to press their legislators to ratify the 19th Amendment.

Four years later, when the 19th Amendment to the U.S. Constitution was ratified by the Pennsylvania General Assembly in June 1919, she became the first woman to ever address the Pennsylvania State Legislature.

She also reportedly presented Pennsylvania's governor with a commemorative gift, which was engraved with a few words about the historic achievement.

During the fall of that same year, Lucy and other leaders of the Pennsylvania Woman Suffrage Association determined that their organization's name should be updated. She became the first president of the League of Women Citizens of Pennsylvania (forerunner of the League of Women Voters of Pennsylvania).

In 1928, Lucy Kennedy Miller and her husband, John Oliver Miller, relocated to Talbot County, Maryland, where they had purchased Emerson Point from the Seth Family in 1928. This did not stop her interest in political and civic matters in Pittsburgh. From the 1930s to the 1950s, Lucy collaborated with her sister, Eliza, to uncover Pittsburgh city government corruption. Exposing the profligate spending and improper city contract awards of Mayor Charles H. Kline, their investigation led to Kline's indictment by a grand jury on forty-eight counts of malfeasance. Convicted in 1932, he received a six-month prison sentence.

Sadly, she was diagnosed with carcinoma of the bowel and died at the age of eighty-one from metastatic bowel cancer on June 30, 1962.

Emerson Point remained in their family and ownership of the historic property was transferred in 1964 to their daughter, Eliza (the subject of this book), who maintained control until her death in 2007.

Eliza Kennedy Smith, Eliza's Aunt (1889–1964)

Eliza Jane Kennedy was born on December 11, 1889, in Latrobe, Pennsylvania, to Julian Kennedy (covered earlier in the book) and Jennie E. Breneman Kennedy.

Julian and Jennie moved the family to Pittsburgh when Eliza, the youngest of the family, was only three years old.

In 1907, at the age of eighteen, she served as the sole attendant for her sister, Lucy, when she married John Oliver Miller. The wedding was held at the Kennedy family's home on Forbes Street in Pittsburgh. Their brothers, J. J. Kennedy, Julian Kennedy, Jr., and Thomas Walker Kennedy, served as three of the groom's seven ushers.

A 1908 graduate of the Winchester Thurston School in Pittsburgh's Shadyside neighborhood, she then studied economics and political science at Vassar College, graduating in 1912.

During her time in school, Eliza, Lucy, and their mother, Jennie, participated in suffrage advocacy training at a school run by Carrie Chapman Catt.

Catt was born in Wisconsin in 1859 and was raised in Iowa. As a youth, she wanted to be a doctor. Catt's father was initially reluctant to allow her to attend college, but he relented, contributing only a part of the costs. To pay her expenses, Catt worked as a dishwasher, an assistant in the school library, and as a teacher at rural schools during school breaks.

Catt joined the Crescent Literary Society, a student organization aimed at advancing student learning skills and self-confidence. Although only men were allowed to speak extemporaneously in meetings, Catt demanded to be allowed to do the same thing. This started a discussion about women's participation in the group and ultimately led to women gaining the right to speak in meetings. This eventually led to her involvement in the women's suffrage movement.

After Catt's training, Eliza, Lucy, and Jennie, took increasingly active roles in the suffrage movement at the city, county, and state levels, marching in suffrage parades, hosting suffrage events for young women, and lobbying state legislators to ratify the 19th Amendment to the U.S. Constitution.

In 1915, Eliza became engaged to Raymond Templeton Smith (1888–1967) a graduate of Cornell who later went on to become an executive vice president of the Pittsburgh Coal Company. Her engagement party, which was held at her family's home on May 17 of that year, became a women's suffrage advocacy night when Lucy called on several of the guests to give brief suffrage speeches.

They subsequently became the parents of sons Templeton Smith (1919–2007), who went on to become one of the first environmental lawyers in America, and Kennedy Smith (1922–1996).

Working with Lucy and fellow suffragists Jennie Bradley Roessing, Mary E. Bakewell, Hannah J. Patterson, and Mary Flinn Lawrence, the group founded the Allegheny County Equal Rights Association (later renamed as the Equal Franchise Federation of Western Pennsylvania) with Lucy serving as the organization's treasurer.

After the 19th Amendment was ratified in June 1919 and leaders of Pennsylvania's suffrage movement determined that suffrage organization names should be updated to reflect their changing mission, the organization became the Equal Franchise Federation of Western Pennsylvania. The Pittsburgh branch formally changed their chapter's name to the Allegheny County League of Women Voters in August 1920 and Eliza subsequently assumed the role of president in 1924. She held that position for decades.

Through the 1930s and 1950s, Eliza and Lucy worked to uncover corruption in the Pittsburgh city government. Their work uncovered untethered spending and improper city contracts under the directions of Mayor Charles H. Kline. Their investigation led to Kline's indictment by a grand jury on forty-eight counts of malfeasance.

In 1963, she was diagnosed with cancer. She was initially cared for at the Presbyterian Hospital in Pittsburgh before she returned to her Squirrel Hill home in the fall of 1964.

She died in her sleep there at the age of seventy-four on October 23, 1964.

The Pittsburgh Press described her as "a relentless, tenacious watchdog of the City's purse strings" who "probably attended more budget sessions over the years than anyone else in Pittsburgh either in or out of government."

James Kennedy, Brother of Eliza's Grandfather, Julian Kennedy (1853–1928)

James was born in 1853 and attended Poland Union Seminary. (This was a Christian school in Poland, Ohio, that taught at a high school and junior college level. It included a dormitory for boys. Girls lived in nearby private housing.) He graduated from Westminster College in 1876, studied law, and was admitted to the bar in 1879. He practiced law in Youngstown, Ohio, was a member of Youngstown City Council from 1886 to 1888, and served as chairman of the Republican Ohio State Convention in 1894. In 1903, he was elected to the U.S. Congress and served until 1911. He resumed his law practice after his time in Congress and continued to practice until his death in 1928.

Hugh Kennedy, Brother of Eliza's Grandfather, Julian Kennedy (1856–1935)

Hugh was awarded a degree from Cooper College in Sterling, Kansas, and acquired his early experience working for his brother, Julian, as an assistant at the furnaces of the Carnegie Steel Company, Braddock, Pennsylvania.

In 1881, he was appointed superintendent and afterward general manager of Isabella Furnaces, Etna, Pennsylvania, where he remained until they were taken over by The American Steel Hoop Company in 1899.

Professionally, he was also the general manager and a director of The Buffalo and Susquehanna Iron Company, the president of the Cascade Coal and Coke Company, and the vice president and director of The Seneca Iron and Steel Company.

He was a member of the American Institute of Mining Engineers.

His activities also included involvement at the civic level. He was president of the Young Men's Christian Association of Buffalo, and member of the board of managers of the Buffalo Historical Society. (My kind of guy.)

He dabbled in golf but was said to take much joy in his children. He and his wife had nine—four sons and five daughters!

Hugh passed away in 1935.

Walter Kennedy, Brother of Eliza's Grandfather, Julian Kennedy (1861–1945)

Walter was born in Ohio in November 1862. While not as well documented as some of his brothers, he worked as a mechanical engineer, and he and his wife, Ann, were the parents to three children.

He died on July 6, 1924, at age sixty-two.

John Harrison Kennedy, Brother of Eliza's Grandfather, Julian Kennedy (1864–1945)

John was born on July 3, 1864, in Ohio. He obtained a degree in chemistry from Geneva College in 1886, and married Edith Hahn in 1893.

By 1899, John was superintendent of the Ironworks in Punxsutawney, Pennsylvania, and in 1912, he moved to Buffalo, New York, to manage the Susquehanna Furnaces of the Rodgers-Brown Iron Company, where his brother, Hugh, was vice president and general manager.

He had retired and moved to East Aurora Village by 1925 and passed away in 1945.

Samuel A. Kennedy, Brother of Eliza's Grandfather, Julian Kennedy (1867–1953)

Samuel was born in 1867 and married Elizabeth Patterson Warner in 1895. They would go on to have three children.

He graduated from Geneva College in 1887 and was an engineer and general manager for the Iroquois Iron and Steel Company in Chicago, Illinois, until 1912.

In 1923, he went to Salt Lake City to consult on the construction of a plant for Columbia Steel Corporation. The family made the town their home, and there he held a variety of positions. He served on the Water District Board of Salt Lake City from its creation in October 1935, and during World War II was a member of Selective Service Board and State Board of Appeals.

He was also involved with the First Security Bank of Utah, the Alta Club, Salt Lake country Club, and United Presbyterian Church.

He passed away on July 28, 1953.

John Knight Shryock, Jr., Son of John and Margurite Shryock, "Adoptive" Parents to Bishop Quentin Huang (1925–1945)

John Shryock was born on December 18, 1925, in China while his parents were serving as missionaries there.

Prior to the start of World War II, his parents returned to the Philadelphia area where John completed his schooling.

He enlisted in the U.S. Army Air Corps on February 12, 1944, in New Cumberland, Pennsylvania, and was assigned to the 400th Bomber Squadron, 90th Bomber Group.

February 1944 was a pivotal time in the war. On the Eastern Front, the Soviet Union was in the midst of a large-scale winter offensive aimed at pushing back German forces from Soviet territory. In Italy, the Allies were facing tough resistance from German forces defending the Gustav Line, a defensive line across central Italy designed to prevent the Allies from advancing toward Rome. Over Europe, the Allied air forces, particularly the U.S. Army Air Forces and the Royal Air Force (RAF), continued their strategic bombing campaign against Nazi Germany. In Western Europe, intense preparation was underway for Operation Overlord, the Allied invasion of Normandy, which would take place in June. Allied commanders, including General Dwight D. Eisenhower, were finalizing plans for the massive amphibious assault, while forces and equipment were being assembled in the United Kingdom. In the Pacific, the United States was advancing across the central Pacific as part of its island-hopping campaign against Japan. At the time, U.S. forces were targeting the Marshall Islands, a strategic group of atolls held by the Japanese.

While the brutal campaign in the Pacific was continuing, on June 6, 1945, John was a passenger aboard the B-24L Liberator #44-41482 when they took off from McGuire Field on Mindoroon. The courier flight was bound for Floridablanca Airfield on Luzon Island, Philippines, with a crew of four along with twenty passengers.

They encountered heavy rain soon after takeoff. They never arrived at their destination and are assumed to have crashed into the sea.

John was declared "Missing in Action." He was just nineteen years old.

At the time of his death, he had achieved the rank of staff sergeant and had been awarded the Air Medal with two Oak Leaf Clusters.

He is memorialized at the Missing Manila American Cemetery Manila, Philippines.

Appendix III
The Pittsburgh Art Scene

130 Gallery

In 1956, Janet and Eliza held a joint show at the 130 Gallery on North Bellefield Avenue in Pittsburgh. At the time, it was one of the most influential galleries in the city and state, and at the heart of the gallery was its founder, Louise Pershing.

Louise was born in 1904 and studied at Carnegie Tech and the University of Pittsburgh in the 1920s. Her instructors included industrial designer Alexander Kostellow, post-impressionist Giovanni Romagnoli, and abstract expressionist Hans Hofmann. Her instructors represented a remarkable array of talent:

Alexander Kostellow, industrial designer (1897–1954)—regarded by many as the "father" of industrial design education—was born in Persia (Iran) as Alexander Jusserand Kostellow. He studied in Paris and at the University of Berlin, and he came to the United States in 1916. In the U.S., Alexander studied painting at the National Academy, the Art Students League, and the Kansas City Art Institute, where he met and married Rowena Reed. Both came to Pittsburgh in 1929 to teach at Carnegie Institute of Technology, he in painting and she in sculpture. By 1934, Alexander and Rowena helped establish the first degreed ID program at Carnegie Tech with co-founder Donald Dohner.

Alexander and Rowena left Pittsburgh in 1938 to join the faculty at the Pratt Institute in Brooklyn.

Giovanni Romagnoli, post-impressionist (1893–1976), was an Italian painter and sculptor born in 1893. He trained at the Academy of Fine Arts of Bologna and specialized in painting female nudes inspired by nineteenth-century painters. He later taught at Carnegie Tech.

Hans Hofmann, abstract expressionist (1880–1966). While not a permanent instructor at Carnegie Tech, Hoffmann's shows and lectures had a profound impact on Louise. Between 1900 and 1930, Hofmann's early studies, decades of painting, and schools of art took him to Munich, to Paris, then back to Munich. By 1933, and for the next four decades, he lived in New York and in Provincetown. Hofmann's life brought him into contact with many of the foremost artists, critics, and dealers of the twentieth century: Henri Matisse, Pablo Picasso, Georges Braque, Wassily Kandinsky, Sonia and

Robert Delaunay, Betty Parsons, Peggy Guggenheim, Lee Krasner, Jackson Pollock, and many others. His career was supported by modern art dealer Sam Kootz, art critic Clement Greenberg, and his first wife, Maria "Miz" Wolfegg (1885–1963).

Louise joined Associated Artists of Pittsburgh in 1927 and embarked on an active professional career that saw her paintings exhibited at institutions and museums around the world.

She was unwavering in her commitment to her artistic visions. In 1934, she painted a 21-foot mural in Hillsdale Elementary School in Dormont in Pittsburgh's Dormont area as a commission from the federal Public Works Administration.

She claimed that the work was a juxtaposition of the life advantages of education against the moral degradation resulting from ignorance. Elements included crime, disease, poverty, gambling, prostitution, revolution, and war. It was not universally popular. The school's parent-teacher association demanded that the mural be removed.

Pershing said: "I consider it a compliment that the people of Dormont feel they cannot accept my mural. That shows it is beyond their intelligence and understanding. If they accepted it readily and with applause, I would doubt if I had created anything worthwhile."

In 1942, her work was recognized with a solo exhibition at the Carnegie Institute Museum of Art which included her landscapes and portraits.

In the 1950s and '60s, Pershing promoted a variety of artists with shows and exhibitions in her 130 Gallery on North Bellefield Avenue, near Carnegie Tech. It was during this time that Janet and Eliza held their joint show.

"She was always trying to promote Pittsburgh artists, and this was one way she could do it," said painter B. G. Galey, a long-time friend.

Her personal artist pursuits turned to sculpture. She began welding found objects together to create a style she called "kinetic sculpture" that merged 3D art with pop art.

Her 1972 abstract steel sculpture *The Flow* remains at the Sixth Street and Bigelow Square in downtown Pittsburgh.

When some voiced their perspective on the work, Pershing said: "I find the ugliness of industrial Pittsburgh is its beauty. Machinery to me is beautiful in its simplicity and precise engineering as compared to the less controlled and directed human being in his striving and searching for an understanding of life and his ability to enjoy it."

Louise was married three times. Twice to New York businessman Datus Berlin and once to Pittsburgh doctor Clifford Murdoch.

She passed away in 1986 at the age of eighty-two.

The Mattress Factory

(Founded by Barbara Luderowski (1930–2018), Janet DeCoux's niece.)

Artistic talent and love of the arts seemed to be a genetic commonality across the DeCoux family. This incredible trait was also found in Janet's niece, Barbara Luderowsky. She was born in New York and raised in Connecticut, but like most people in this story, her journey included a Pittsburgh chapter—or two.

She studied at Carnegie Tech, then the Art Students League of New York, and, finally, the Cranbrook Academy of Art in Michigan. While at Cranbrook, she married the school's design teacher Ted Luderowski. She then went on to work at an architectural firm and as a designer at General Motors. In her spare time, she pursued her own artistic passions.

After the death of her husband in 1972, Barbara approached the Pittsburgh History & Landmarks Foundation about a garden she wanted to design for them. That project fell through, but she became enamored with the city's North Side neighborhood. Barbara said: "... it was like seeing someone across the room at a cocktail party and saying, 'That's for me.' So I went home to Birmingham, Mich., put my house up for sale, and bought a house here."

She moved into a very rough home on Monterey Street in the Mexican War Streets neighborhood with her daughter who was ten at the time. While Barbara saw the possibilities, her daughter did not. Barbara recalled: "Pieces of the floor were missing. You had to tippy-toe your way through. The only light was either your flashlight or light peeping through some of the knot-holes. But I don't walk into houses and see the crap. I see what I want to make out of them. My daughter, however, took one look at what was going to be her bedroom and burst into tears."

She and her daughter saw the project to its completion. "I designed and, in some cases, did the carpentry and laid some of the floors, along with a bunch of Carnegie-Mellon architecture students," Barbara said. The project sparked in her a desire to explore the possibilities of older properties.

A few years later, Luderowski bought a former mattress warehouse at 500 Sampsonia Way in Pittsburgh. She wanted to make it a center for artists and thinkers. It eventually became her live/workspace, as well as a building that housed studios for artists, a food co-op, and a theater. In 1977, Barbara turned it into a nonprofit educational center with a directorial board, and the Mattress Factory was born. The museum staged its first exhibition only five years later.

Barbara recalled:

> The intention I had at the time, as best I can reconstruct it, was to create my own environment. When I first moved to Pittsburgh, the city was incredibly conservative. In those days, there was a place called the King Pitcher Gallery on Craig Street, which was handling my work. There, I met artists at various meetings and openings. But I really wanted a place with some real vitality, where there was intellectual exchange, a mishmash of various disciplines with energetic conversation, and I couldn't find that anywhere. So I set about trying to create that.

Since those early days, the Mattress Factory has bought and fixed up eight other properties in the area. The artistic mission has supported the work of more than 600 artists in residence, and hosted exhibitions by Janine Antoni, Jessica Stockholder, Cady Noland, Charles Ray, William Anastasi, and Vito Acconci, among many others.

The museum welcomes about 28,400 visitors annually and serves a community of 47,700 patrons via membership, educational initiatives, and other programs.

Barbara passed away in 2018, but when considering her role in the Pittsburgh art scene, her death does not feel like the end of the story.

"I talk mostly about what's now—and the future. It takes a lot of time and energy to talk about the past. It's much more interesting for me to talk about what you want to do, what you like to do, and where you'd like to go than it is to talk about where you've been. I face forward and go forward."

Appendix IV

More Amazing Places Connected to This Story

The Father of Our Country, An Outlaw, and The Underground Railroad—All in Gibsonia

In addition to being the home of Janet DeCoux, Eliza Miller, and Bishop Quentin Huang, Richland Township, which includes Gibsonia, is also the site of several other historic events.

In 1753, George Washington, who was only twenty-one at the time, was given a mission by the governor of Virginia to take a message to Fort Le Boeuf in Erie, Pennsylvania.

Washington and eleven other men, including surveyor Christopher Gist, left the Ohio River about 20 miles downstream from Pittsburgh and headed north on November 30, 1753. They made it to the fort, but after that, history gets a little cloudy. Traditional recountings of the tale said they returned via the same path. New research shows they took a different route—one that took them through Richland Township.

Twenty years later, another notable character was prowling the woods of Richland, but he was notable for all the wrong reasons.

Simon Girty was born in 1741 near Harrisburg, Pennsylvania, and at the age of fourteen, he was taken from his home by Shawnee Indians and later given to the Seneca of the Iroquois Nation. Even though he was of Irish and Scottish descent, Girty assimilated with the native tribes, spending over seven years participating in Indian warfare. In 1764, Girty was returned to Pittsburgh's Fort Pitt, where he served the British Army as an interpreter.

Between 1760 and 1790, a group of outlaws made up of Simon and his brothers, James and George, along with a number of Delaware, Shawnee, Mingo, and Wynadot Indians set up camp in Gibsonia. The hill they chose was known as "Girty's Knob" which was just a mile south of Janet and Eliza's home which was built just a few decades later in the 1840s. The Girtys roamed the area, terrorizing white settlers and peddling their scalps to the British for $10 apiece.

Girty left Pennsylvania for loyalist Detroit in 1778, returning briefly to Pittsburgh in 1792. When Detroit came under U.S. control, he moved to Canada, where he died in 1818. He was said to be financially destitute and nearly blind.

Just a few decades later, another series of crimes were taking place in the area; these were the very best kind. In the decades leading up to the Civil War, many southern slaves escaped to freedom using the Underground Railroad. This became even more difficult in 1850 when a federal law required free states to help return runaway slaves.

Less than a mile from Janet and Eliza's home, the Tom and Rosanna Henry Farmhouse (more recently called Walnut Knoll) served as a stop on the Underground Railroad. The home's location far back from the road made a wonderfully discrete hiding spot.

All of this leads to the obvious question: what other history is hiding in the area?

The Burma Road

Relations between China and Japan had been tumultuous for generations, and the impact of the First Sino-Japanese War (1894–1895) was still being felt by the time Bishop Huang was born in 1902. Famine, taxation, and economic hardship endured through the 1920s and 1930s.

By the 1930s, relations were strained again, and the Second Sino-Japanese War began between the Republic of China and the Empire of Japan in 1937.

As Japan began an aggressive expansion into East Asia, China began losing control of its ports. The Chinese Nationalist government knew that an open supply line was necessary. The solution was to build a road connecting Kunming in China's Yunnan province to Lashio in Burma. In total, the road would be more than 700 miles long when constructed. The project was considered a monumental engineering feat, given the challenging terrain of mountains, jungles, and rivers. The strength of human resolve was a significant part as well. The construction employed hundreds of thousands of Chinese laborers, often working under harsh conditions with minimal machinery. The labor force faced numerous challenges, including rugged landscapes, inclement weather, and diseases such as malaria. Despite these obstacles, the road was completed in just over a year.

As Japanese forces intensified their campaigns, the road became vitally significant. With Chinese ports under Japanese control, the road offered a lifeline for military supplies and other essential goods. It connected with the Ledo Road (later known as the Stilwell Road) in India, creating an overland supply route that circumvented Japanese naval blockades.

With the outbreak of World War II, the Burma Road emerged as a critical supply route for the Allies. It facilitated the flow of military equipment, food, and medical supplies from British-controlled Burma to the Chinese forces resisting Japanese invasion.

The road saw its first major use in 1938 when the Chinese government began transporting supplies, particularly after the fall of Guangzhou and Wuhan to the Japanese. Trucks loaded with arms, ammunition, and other military essentials navigated the treacherous route, bolstering the Chinese war effort.

The strategic value of the Burma Road did not go unnoticed by the Japanese military. In 1940, Japan exerted diplomatic pressure on the British government to close the road. This led to a temporary closure, but the road was reopened in October 1940 due to the pressing need to support China.

The United States played a pivotal role in utilizing and enhancing the Burma Road. After the attack on Pearl Harbor in December 1941, the U.S. recognized the importance of maintaining China as an active participant in the war against Japan. American aid, including the Lend-Lease program, began to flow through the Burma Road, reinforcing Chinese resistance.

The road's rugged terrain and harsh weather conditions posed significant logistical challenges. Landslides, flooding, and maintenance issues frequently disrupted the flow of supplies. The road's narrow and winding nature limited the volume of traffic, necessitating careful coordination and planning.

Japanese forces made concerted efforts to disrupt the supply route. Air raids, sabotage, and ground assaults targeted key points along the road, necessitating constant vigilance and defense by Allied forces. The threat of Japanese interference added an additional layer of complexity to the operation of the road.

The allocation of resources to the construction and maintenance of the Burma Road and the Ledo Road diverted manpower, equipment, and materials from other fronts. Balancing the needs of the CBI theater with the broader demands of the global war effort required careful strategic planning.

Recognizing the limitations of the Burma Road, the Allies initiated the construction of the Ledo Road in 1942, named after its starting point in Ledo, India. Under the direction of General Joseph Stilwell, this project aimed to create an alternative route that would connect with the Burma Road at the China–Burma border. The Ledo Road traversed some of the most inhospitable terrains in the world, including dense jungles, steep mountains, and swift rivers.

The construction of the Ledo Road presented formidable engineering challenges. The terrain required extensive use of bulldozers, dynamite, and innovative engineering techniques. Allied engineers, including American, British, Indian, and Chinese personnel, worked tirelessly to overcome these obstacles. The road featured numerous bridges, culverts, and switchbacks to navigate the difficult landscape.

The Ledo Road was completed in early 1945 and integrated with the Burma Road, significantly enhancing the capacity and efficiency of the overland supply route. The combined route, now often referred to as the Stilwell Road, facilitated the transportation of vast quantities of supplies, including trucks, fuel, weapons, and medical equipment, to Chinese forces.

The Burma Road, along with the Ledo Road, had a profound impact on the Allied war effort in the China–Burma–India (CBI) theater. The supply route was instrumental in sustaining Chinese resistance against Japanese aggression. The flow of military supplies enabled Chinese forces to launch counter offensives and maintain a protracted defense. This, in turn, tied down significant Japanese military resources that could have been deployed elsewhere in the Asia–Pacific region.

The existence of the Burma Road provided the Allies with strategic flexibility. It allowed for the movement of troops and equipment across the theater, facilitating coordinated operations against Japanese forces in Burma and beyond. The road also served as a conduit for intelligence and communication, enhancing the overall coordination of Allied efforts.

After the war, the Burma Road continued to serve as a vital transportation route in the region. Its construction laid the groundwork for post-war infrastructure development, contributing to economic growth and regional connectivity. The road's existence facilitated trade and communication between Burma and China, fostering closer ties between the two nations.

Cranbrook, Where Janet and Eliza Met Anne Morrow Lindberg

The Cranbrook Academy of Art was founded by George Gough Booth and his wife, Ellen Scripps Booth, in the early twentieth century.

Ellen was born in 1863, and her father, James E. Scripps, was the founder of *The Detroit News*. Her uncle, E. W. Scripps, founded the E. W. Scripps Company, a major media conglomerate.

George Gough Booth was born on September 24, 1864. His father, Henry Wood Booth, was an inventor and businessman, and George began working at his father's printing business at a young age.

In 1893, George married Ellen and joined *The Detroit News*, where he worked in various capacities and eventually rose to become a key figure in the newspaper's operations. Under his leadership, *The Detroit News* became one of the leading newspapers in the Midwest.

The couple held a truly prominent position among the highest echelons of Detroit's elite.

Inspired by the Arts and Crafts movement and driven by a desire to create an educational community that emphasized artistic craftsmanship and interdisciplinary learning, the Booths purchased a large tract of land in Bloomfield Hills in 1904.

Initially, the land was developed into a family estate, but the Booths kept their focus on their ambitious plans, and those plans took shape over the following years.

Eliel Saarinen (1873–1950) was teaching architecture at the University of Michigan when he caught the attention of the Booths, whose son, Henry, was one of Saarinen's architecture students. Saarinen's resume was impressive. He was already well established as an architect in Finland when, in 1922, he entered a competition to design the *Chicago Tribune* building. He won second place and used the prize money to immigrate to Chicago in 1923, eventually joined by his wife, Loja (1879–1968); daughter, Pipsan (1905–1979); and son, Eero (1910–1961).

The Booths engaged Saarinen as chief architect for the campus, and he ultimately designed Cranbrook School for boys (1925–1929), Kingswood School for girls (1929–1931), Cranbrook Institute of Science (1935–1938), Cranbrook Academy of Art (1925–1942), and Cranbrook Art Museum and Library (1938–1942).

The academy officially opened in 1932, initially offering programs in architecture, painting, and sculpture. Saarinen formulated the academy's curriculum and served as its first president from 1932–1946, headed its Department of Architecture and Urban Design from 1932–1950, and designed numerous non-Cranbrook commissions. His wife, Loja, also contributed significantly, particularly in the field of textile design.

Cranbrook's unique educational model, which eschewed traditional grades and rigid curricula in favor of a more open and mentor-based approach, allowed for significant artistic innovation. Students were encouraged to explore their creative boundaries, engage in interdisciplinary projects, and develop their individual artistic voices.

When the Lindberg family moved to Detroit so Charles could supervise the production of bombers in World War II, Anne Morrow Lindberg began taking classes at Cranbrook. While she was one of the most famous people in the world at the time, others became legendary in the field of design—all shaped by Cranbrook, including Charles and Ray Eames, Harry Bertoia, Florence Knoll, Jack Lenor Larsen, Donald

Lipski, Duane Hanson, Lorraine Wild, Nick Cave, Hani Rashid, and, of course, Janet DeCoux and Eliza Miller.

In the latter half of the twentieth century and into the twenty-first century, Cranbrook Academy of Art continued to evolve, adapting to changes in the art world while maintaining its commitment to fostering creativity and innovation. The academy expanded its programs to include contemporary fields such as digital art, new media, and critical studies. The institution also remained committed to its core values of craftsmanship, interdisciplinary learning, and artistic excellence. The campus itself continued to serve as a living work of art, with ongoing efforts to preserve and enhance its architectural and natural beauty.

Today, Cranbrook Academy of Art is recognized as a premier institution for graduate-level education in art, design, and architecture.

Rhode Island School of Design

A number of people throughout this story spent time studying at the Rhode Island School of Design. The founding of the institution can be traced to Heled Adelia Row Metcalf. She was born Helen Adelia Rowe in Providence Rhode Island in 1830. At the age of twenty-two, she married Jesse Metcalf, a southern cotton buyer who later co-founded the Wanskuck Company in 1862.

In 1877, Helen and a group of Providence women attended the Centennial Exposition in Philadelphia. At the exposition, she was particularly fascinated by the Women's Pavilion organized by a group called "Centennial Women," which showcased the work of female entrepreneurs, artists, and designers.

Upon returning to Rhode Island, Metcalf lobbied the local committee of Centennial Women to use $1,675 in funds they had to establish a co-education design school on Providence. In January 1877, the committee voted to approve Metcalf's proposal. Just a few months later, the Rhode Island General Assembly ratified "An Act to Incorporate the Rhode Island School of Design," "or the purpose of aiding in the cultivation of the arts of design."

Metcalf passed away in 1895, but the institution was growing with both expanded curriculum and facilities. It also developed new programs and enhanced existing ones to adapt to changing trends in art and design education. The institution gained more recognition and accreditation, solidifying its reputation as a premier art and design school in the United States.

A museum also took shape, and by the 1920s, the museum's collection grew significantly due to gifts and an expanding endowment. This allowed the museum to purchase major artworks and expand physically. In 1924, the Metcalfe Building was added.

In 1932, under the leadership of President Helen Metcalf Danforth, Helen's granddaughter, the school was granted the right to grant college degrees instead of certificates. RISD became a fully accredited college in 1949. The students of the Rhode Island School of Design have left their mark on a wide spectrum of artistic endeavors.

Painting and the visual arts:

- Kara Walker, renowned contemporary artist known for her silhouette work.
- Nicole Eisenman, painter and sculptor.
- Shepard Fairey, street artist and graphic designer famous for the "OBEY" campaign and Obama "Hope" poster.

Industrial and graphic design:

- Brian Chesky, co-founder and CEO of Airbnb.
- Joe Gebbia, co-founder of Airbnb and chairman of Airbnb's design studio.

Film and television:

- Seth MacFarlane, creator of *Family Guy* and other animated series.
- Gus Van Sant, acclaimed film director known for indie and mainstream films.
- Michael Dante DiMartino, co-creator of *Avatar: The Last Airbender* and *The Legend of Korra*.

Music:

- David Byrne, lead singer of Talking Heads (attended but did not graduate).
- Chris Frantz and Tina Weymouth, members of Talking Heads (attended as freshmen).

Architecture:

- Deborah Berke, dean of Yale School of Architecture and principal of Deborah Berke Partners.

Other notable alumni:

- Dale Chihuly, renowned glass artist.
- Jemima Kirke, actress known for her role in the TV series *Girls*.
- James Franco, actor, filmmaker, and artist (attended but unclear if graduated).

Emerson Point, The Family Home of the Millers

Dr. James Seth was born in 1843. He married Sydney Maria Orem and became a successful businessman in Maryland, serving as the director for the Eastern National Bank. Sadly, his wife Sydney passed away just five days after the birth of their first daughter in 1871. She was only twenty-six.

He would marry again. His new wife was Julia Taylor Orem, Sydney's sister. They would go on to have six more children together.

Dr. Seth was very active in real estate, and over the years he accumulated large land holdings, including a large tract of land 60 miles southwest of Baltimore on the Eastern Bay of the Chesapeake Bay called Emerson Point in Talbot County, Maryland.

The land was the site of several structures, two thought to be boarding houses, and a mid-nineteenth-century cemetery was also located on the site, containing graves of both white and African American individuals. It was long rumored that Frederick Douglas spent time on Emerson Point. A large, stately home was later built on the property.

Dr. Seth passed away in 1901 and was remembered not only for his business accomplishments, but for his civic endeavors as well.

Julia Seth, his second wife, passed away in 1926.

In 1928, Lucy Kennedy Miller and her husband, John Oliver Miller, relocated to Maryland, after purchasing Emerson Point from the Seth Family in 1928. The family enjoyed the expansive property for years, and Peter Shefler, Eliza's nephew, spent a significant portion of his life there.

A survey by the Maryland Historical Trust conducted in 2004 recorded a "house built in 1928 in the Georgian Revival style, and an overseer's house."

The family enjoyed a warm relationship with Leslie Newman who served as a caretaker for the property. Peter Shefler referred to him as "my dear friend and a father to me."

Ownership of the historic property was transferred in 1964 to their daughter, Eliza Jane Miller, who maintained control until her death in 2007.

Emerson Point still stands and continues to be recognized for its historical significance. It has been documented not only by the Maryland Historical Trust, but other historical organizations as well.

Note: Sara Seth, the daughter of Dr. James Seth and Julie Orem Seth, would later marry Raymond Clark. The Clark Estate gifted a number of photos to the Talbot County Historical Society in Maryland showing the early days of Emerson Point when it was owned by the Seth family.

A historical photo of Emerson Point. Date unknown.

The Butler Plank Road

In the early 1800s, America was still a largely rural and agrarian society with scattered towns and villages and very few established routes. This was especially true in the "western" part of the country which included western Pennsylvania, Ohio, and Indiana. Existing roads were little more than rough trails and were prone to mud, floods, and erosion. Bridges were virtually non-existent, and ascending and descending hills was treacherous. Most routes followed paths established by Native Americans in previous generations or followed paths created by traders, trappers, and settlers. Travel was slow and unreliable.

Steamboats and canals alleviated part of this issue, but western Pennsylvania, with the exclusion of its three famous rivers, lacked navigable rivers, streams, and lakes.

In western Pennsylvania, a need to connect Pittsburgh and the northern city of Butler was evident. The two were linked by an Indian trace the width of a horse. It was neither efficient nor practical.

The first attempt at an improved road came in 1804 when the state government approved improvements to the existing trail. The upgrades were limited to removing trees, stumps, and underbrush.

The Pitttsburgh and Butler Turnpike Company was formed in 1819, and by 1822, some sections were open. (The term "turnpike" originated from the early toll road systems in England and colonial America, where roads were often blocked by a gate or barrier, called a "pike" or "turnpike." This barrier would turn or pivot open once a traveler or vehicle paid a toll.)

In order to build the road, contracts were given for 5 and 10-mile segments. In total, the road covered nearly 32 miles and included seventeen bridges.

The route began on Federal Street in Allegheny City (now Pittsburgh's North Side), ran east, and then followed what is now Route 28 to Etna, a borough upstream along the Allegheny river from downtown Pittsburgh.

From there, the road headed north and then connected to what is now Route 8 near Wildwood. The road was not paved. Only a surface of clay was used to smooth the surface.

While the turnpike did provide a route for goods and travelers, the income generated from the tolls did not cover the costs of maintenance, and the road fell into disrepair. In 1850, investors assembled, and the new Allegheny and Butler Plank Road Company was incorporated in February 1851. William Dickey (he was the source of the name of the road on which Janet and Eliza lived) and Richard Morrow were awarded contracts for sections of the road.

Although rough and crude by some standards, plank roads were considered modern by the day's standards. The plank road concept was gaining traction across the United States inspired by similar models in Europe, particularly in Russia and the Netherlands. Plank roads consisted of a layer of wooden planks laid over a roadbed, creating a smoother and more durable surface than traditional dirt roads. Given the abundance of timber in Pennsylvania, this was an ideal solution.

The Butler Plank Road had a base of crushed flagstone, covered with hand-split logs. The new road was finished in 1853 at a cost of $116,000. The first record of tolls appears to be in 1855, with tolls amounting to $9,030.64. The cost of travel was 2 cents per mile for a horse and 3½ cents for a team, except on Sundays when travel was free.

The venture was successful and even upgraded in the 1870s when the split logs were replaced by factory sawn planks.

Its success would not last forever. The Pennsylvania weather was hard on the road. Planks warped, rotted, and broke. Heavy usage, while good for revenue, increased the wear on the road. When maintenance fell behind, dissatisfaction rose. As railroads extended more tracks into the area, the need for the road fell. Railroads were both faster and cheaper. Eventually the road was abandoned.

In 1905, the southern half of the road was sold to Allegheny County for $65,000, while the Butler portion of the road was taken over by the state in 1913.

The current Route 8 appeared in 1918 serving the role of connecting Pittsburgh to Butler. It was upgraded in 1921 and again in 1934. By the 1950s, it was a four-lane highway.

Saint Thomas in the Fields Church stands on a knoll overlooking Route 8. If you happen to be stopped by the traffic light, you'll have time to reflect on the bell tower created by Janet DeCoux.

Acknowledgments

This book started with a walk through my old neighborhood and a lot of questions. Early in the process I was able to locate and talk with several people who provided enough clues to jumpstart my research.

Alice Huang, the bishop's daughter—I cannot imagine what she thought when I called her out the blue. She was a great help in giving me details about her father's life, and although she could not recall their names, she knew that "two artists" helped him greatly when he built his home. She was also able to provide numerous images for this book.

The Staff of Saint Thomas in the Fields—The staff was able to make the historical connection between Janet, Eliza, and the bishop. They also provided some documents about the history of the church which helped provide more background for the story.

Peter Sheffler, Eliza's nephew—Peter was a great help in providing the human context around Janet and Eliza. He was also able to provide some details around the bishop. Additionally, he provided many images for this book.

Reverend David Knox—Reverend Knox of Trinity Episcopal Church in Mattoon, Illinois, was able to provide details about the early work of Janet's father.

My father, Edward C. Weiss—My father has always been immensely curious about history and his recollection of facts and stories is amazing. The details of the bishop's home, to this point, have always been a blank spot in the history of our neighborhood. I am looking forward to my father adding this story to his list of stories.